Design History

After Germany was defeated in World War One, the victorious powers were determined that Germany would not be a future military threat to them and imposed very restrictive terms in the Versailles Peace Treaty of 1919. When it came to the German Navy, new German battleships could not exceed 10,000 tons, a measure designed to restrict Germany to small coast defence capital ships. When it came to cruisers the maximum displacement of any new German cruiser design was limited to 6000 tons and maximum gun size to 6in. These limitations allowed construction of satisfactory smaller cruisers with a scout mission but precluded designs comparable to the heavier cruiser designs of the major naval powers. In both cases German new construction was confined to replacing existing vessels when they reached twenty years of age. However, this last restriction had only a minimal impact as Germany was allowed to keep only her oldest battleships and cruisers.

Under the terms of the Washington Naval Treaty of 1922 the world's major naval powers agreed to limit themselves in future warship construction to avoid the new naval arms race that had been developing. The major impact of the Treaty was in the area of battleship construction, which put a limit on individual ship design, as well as imposing a total tonnage cap on every major nation's battlefleet. However, cruiser design was also covered in the Treaty, with maximum displacement limited to 10,000 tons and maximum gun size to 8in. Great Britain had been a strong advocate of these parameters as it allowed the Royal Navy to retain the *Hawkins* class cruisers built at the end of the war which displaced slightly below the 10,000-ton limit and which were armed with 7.5in guns. However, there were no limits on total cruiser tonnage and a new arms race broke out in cruiser construction with the Treaty-imposed maximum displacement and maximum gun size becoming the accepted norm. At this time there was no distinction between heavy and light cruisers, as all new construction was typed as light cruiser regardless of displacement or gun size. This distinguished them from the handful of battlecruisers still around (which were subject to capital ship restrictions) and the obsolete armoured cruisers produced before the introduction of the battlecruiser. For the time being this was of no relevance to Germany, as she was not a signatory to

The launching ceremony for *Admiral Hipper*, 6 February 1937, at Blohm & Voss, Hamburg. The ship was christened by Admiral Raeder's wife.

DESIGN CHARACTERISTICS

Dimensions	*Hipper/Blücher*: Length 675ft 4ins (205.9m) oa; 636ft 9ins (194.6m) wl. Beam 69ft 9ins (21.3m). Draught 19ft (5.83m) mean *Prinz Eugen*: Length 690ft 7ins (212.5m) oa; 654ft 4ins (199.5m) wl. Beam 71ft 9ins (21.9m). Draught 20ft 9ins (6.37m) mean
Displacement	14,247 tons standard; 18,208 tons full load for *Hipper* 14,475 tons standard; 18,500 tons full load for *Blücher* 16,277 tons standard; 18,960 tons full load for *Prinz Eugen*
Armament	Eight 8in (203mm) guns (4x2); twelve 4.1in (105mm) heavy AA guns (6x2); twelve 37mm medium AA guns (6x2); eight 20mm light AA guns (8x1)
Vertical Armour	Main belt 70-80mm; conning tower 50-150mm; main turrets 70-105mm
Horizontal Armour	Main deck armoured deck 20-50mm; upper armoured deck 12-30mm
Machinery	Three high-pressure turbines; twelve small water tube boilers, 133,631shp. Speed 32.5kts maximum

Blücher in the final phase of fitting out at Deutsche Werke Yard, Kiel, sometime late in 1938. The main armament and torpedo tubes are on board, but the lighter weapons have still to be fitted.

the Naval Treaty, and was in any case confined by the far more restrictive terms of the Treaty of Versailles.

Under these terms the first cruiser which could be replaced was *Ariadne*, which reached twenty years of age in 1921. Since the end of the war Germany had descended into chaos. With crushing reparation payments and the beginnings of hyper-inflation, the Weimar Republic had little money or inclination to rebuild her navy. German naval designers looked to the last classes of cruisers produced for the Imperial German Navy, which were rather good designs. As a consequence the design for this first post-war cruiser was essentially a World War One design. Although twin centreline 5.9in (150mm) gun mountings were considered, the final design reverted to open gun mounts with splinter shields and retention of obsolete broadside guns. The propulsion was just as obsolescent with mixed oil- and coal-fired boilers, producing a maximum speed of 29 knots – clearly slower than her contemporaries. Displacing 5600 tons, the *Emden* was the only German cruiser which met the 6000-ton displacement limit, but from first commissioning on 15 October 1925 the *Emden* was slated for training duties to educate the personnel of a reborn German Navy. With their next cruiser design, there would be a clear break from World War One designs for the German naval architects.

The next design tried to do too much on the 6000-ton displacement limit, and the resulting three-ship *Königsberg* or K class, all laid down in 1926, was a clear failure, with significant weakness caused by overloading the design. Mounting three triple 5.9in turrets, and capable of 32kts, the design initially appeared to be clearly superior to the *Emden*. To save weight, extensive use was made of electrical welding in place of heavier rivet construction, but the price paid for these capabilities was questionable hull strength. Even with weight saving measures, the *Königsberg* design displaced 6650 tons, exceeding the 6000-ton Treaty limitation by 10 per cent. This set the pattern of the Weimar Republic concealing the true displacement of their warships, which became the standard practice of the succeeding Third Reich. The final two '6000-ton' cruisers, the *Leipzig* of 1928 and the *Nürnberg* of 1933 were improvements to the *Konigsberg* design, with basically similar performance characteristics.

Admiral Hipper on her commissioning day, 29 April 1939. The ship demonstrates the original design, with a straight stem (and stemhead crest), a flat-topped funnel, and the open admiral's bridge, all unsatisfactory features that were quickly modified in this and succeeding ships.

Blücher shortly after commissioning, in September or October 1939, at Kiel. The ship already sports the clipper-shaped *Atlantik* bow and a funnel cap.

In 1930 the heavy cruiser, as a formal type, made its first appearance. In the cruiser role the Royal Navy needed quantity not individual ship quality, but having set the design characteristics of inter-war cruiser construction in order to save the completing 'Elizabethans', Great Britain found herself hoist by her own petard. Still not recovered from the financial ruin caused by the expenditures of the war, the government pared down construction requests in the name of economy. Great Britain simply could not afford to match the United States and Imperial Japan on a ship-for-ship basis and ceased construction of 10,000-ton cruisers in favour of smaller but more numerous cruisers. Afraid of falling further behind the other two world powers, the British government called for a new naval armaments reduction conference, which resulted in the London Treaty of 1930. The cruiser was divided into two types: light cruisers were limited to 6.1in guns, while the new heavy cruiser designation covered any ship mounting guns of 8in down to 6.2in. Both types were still limited to 10,000 tons standard displacement, but caps were placed on total cruiser tonnage within each sub-category. As with the Washington negotiations nine years earlier, Germany was not invited to the London conference. Nonetheless German admirals were following developments with interest.

Shortly after the London Treaty was signed, Germany began preparation of her next cruiser design. However, this time the design was based on a treaty-breaking 10,000 tons, rather than just fudging the 6000-ton Versailles limitation. Although the admirals realised that Germany could not yet build a heavy cruiser, it was decided in the early 1930s to prepare for that day with design studies for the type. By February 1934 parameters were established to require that a new cruiser design had to be more powerful than the French heavy cruiser *Algerie*, faster than the French battleship *Dunkerque* with a required 33kts, and with large range, capable of operations in the Atlantic. In a nod to the

The *Prinz Eugen* on 31 July 1940, in the final stages of fitting out. Both main directors have their radar antennas fitted, but they are shrouded in canvas, as are the searchlights and other pieces of equipment.

The forward turrets of *Prinz Eugen* during Baltic trials early in 1940. Designated Drh LC/34, the turrets varied in shape, the superfiring mounts containing a 7-metre rangefinder that required the turret height to be increased and the angled front to be extended to meet a shortened roof.

restrictions of the London Treaty, which Germany had not signed, maximum displacement was to be no more than 10,700 tons. There was a division of thought when it came to main armament and propulsion. One concept called for four twin 8in (203mm) gun turrets, while another called for four triple gun 5.9in (150mm) turrets. The chief discussion point revolved around the fact that a 5.9in gunned ship could be slightly smaller and lighter. Brief consideration was given to a different design with eight 7.48in (190mm) guns, which was quickly rejected. The final decision was to produce the 8in gun design.

When it came to a propulsion plant, there were also divided opinions. The *panzerschiffe* design for *Deutschland* had employed diesel engines to provide extremely long range, but although fuel-efficient, the diesel plant could not provide high speed. A turbo electric plant was briefly considered but in the end a high-pressure steam turbine plant was selected. It was this propulsion system that would become the Achilles' heel of the class. The initial armour scheme called for the design to have belt and barbette armour of 85mm, turret armour of 120mm, and a 30mm armoured deck, except over the steering gear and magazine where the thickness was increased to 50mm. In October 1934 in an effort to save weight the armour thickness was reduced. Maximum belt thickness was reduced to 80mm, maximum deck armour dropped to 40mm but the 30mm general standard was retained. Even with the reduction in armour, the design still exceeded the Washington Treaty 10,000-ton limitation, never mind that the Treaty of Versailles which still limited Germany to 6000-ton cruisers. In that same month, even without a final design, an order was placed with Deutsche Werke for the first ship of the class (*Blücher*).

The main armament of the new cruiser class was the 8in/60 SKC/43, which could reach nearly 40,000 yards at a maximum elevation of 37 degrees. These are the after turrets of *Blücher*, during sea trials in the Baltic, March 1940.

On 16 March 1935 Hitler abrogated the Treaty of Versailles and there was no international response. Now the secrecy could be abandoned and construction of the new cruiser started. In April 1935 an order for the second ship of the class was awarded to Blohm and Voss (*Admiral Hipper*). After the abrogation of the Versailles Treaty, Great Britain quickly negotiated an agreement with Germany that restricted the German Navy to 35 per cent of the strength of the Royal Navy by type and that Germany comply with the restrictions of the Washington Treaty. The agreement was signed on 18 June 1935. Under the terms of the new agreement Germany could have 50,000 tons of heavy cruisers. With only two ordered, this left the option to build

ARMAMENT CHARACTERISTICS

Ordnance	Purpose	Horizontal Range	Elevation/Vertical Range	Rate of Fire RPM	Shell Weight
8in (203mm)/ 60 SKC/34	Surface fire	39,850yds; 36,440m	37 degrees/NA	3	250lbs; 122kg
4.1in (105mm)/L65	DP but primarily heavy AA	19,357yds; 17,700m	85 degrees/ 12,500m	15	33.3lbs; 15.1kg
40mm (1.58in) Bofors Flak 28	Medium AA	11,000yds; 10,000m	?/7000m	120 maximum	2lbs; 0.955kg
37mm (1.46in) / L83 SK C30	Medium AA	7382yds; 6750m effective	80 degrees/6800m maximum/ 4800m effective	160 maximum; 60 operational	1.64lbs; 0.745kg
20mm (0.79in)	Light AA	5249yds; 4800m	90 degrees/4800m maximum/ 3700m effective	280 maximum; 120 operational	0.291lb; 0.132kg
21in (533mm) torpedo tubes	Sub-surface	6000m at 44kts 8000m at 40kts 14,000m at 30kts	NA	NA – 10 reloads (12 for *Prinz Eugen*)	1,538kg

Above: A quarter view of *Admiral Hipper* late in April 1940 at Wilhelmshaven. With topmast struck, the ship is in drydock for repairs to the damage caused by being rammed by HMS *Glowworm* earlier that month.

Left: *Admiral Hipper* cleaning guns, off France, in mid 1941, after battle practice. The guns now have more prominent blast bags. Note the camouflage on the superstructure and the swastika on the foredeck, with its pattern carried over the anchor chains.

three more. On 16 November 1935 a third ship of the class was ordered from Krupp (*Prinz Eugen*).

In 1936 the major naval powers again met in London for discussions on a new naval agreement to replace the London Treaty of 1930. Originally Germany was to have participated but France blocked this move, arguing that to allow Germany to participate was tantamount to recognising that the Treaty of Versailles no longer bound Germany – even though Great Britain had already done just that the year before with the Anglo-German naval agreement. One outcome of the conference was to forbid any further heavy cruiser or capital ship construction. Realising that Germany would not be bound by the terms of any new treaty, the British government quickly negotiated a side deal which allowed Germany to build two further *panzerschiffen* (*Scharnhorst* and *Gneisenau*) and more heavy cruisers, but only under the rather nebulous condition of 'press of exceptional circumstances'. This threw German designers completely off track, as there had been no significant work on a 10,000-ton ship with 5.9in guns, along the lines of the Royal Navy *Southampton* class or the USN *Brooklyn* class. The initial design called for long range, a robust armour scheme, and a 35kt maximum speed. The requirements could not be met within any reasonable displacement. Raeder went back to the heavy cruiser design but with triple 5.9in turrets replacing the twin 8in turrets. On 18 July 1936 an order for two of these light cruisers was placed with Deschimag (*Seydlitz* and *Lützow*). This unforeseen detour ended in November when Hitler invoked the vague 'exceptional circumstances' clause and ordered the last two ships to be completed as heavy cruisers.

The original design used for the first two ships, *Blücher* and *Hipper*, was far in excess of the Treaty maximum displacement of 10,000 tons, coming in at 14,247 tons standard. Even though *Blücher* was first to be ordered, *Hipper* was the first of the class to be laid down, on 6 July 1935, followed on 15 August 1935 by *Blücher*. *Hipper* was launched on 6 February 1937, followed by her sister on 8 June 1937. *Hipper* was completed on 29 April 1939, the only one of the class to be finished before World War Two, although *Blücher* completed shortly after its outbreak, on 20 September 1939.

Prinz Eugen was subject to a change of design, after it became clear that in *Hipper* and *Blücher* the machinery spaces were cramped. As a consequence, each of the machinery spaces was lengthened by .75m to 1.25m, reducing congestion, as well as lengthening the hull from 675ft (205.9m) to 690ft (212.5m) overall (after fitting the

Admiral Hipper conducting trials off the coast of France in mid 1941. A single 20mm gun has been added atop Caesar turret. The ship's floatplane is airborne and can be seen head-on between the barrels of the turrets.

Admiral Hipper at Cuxhaven in April 1940 embarking troops for *Weserübung*, the invasion of Norway.

Atlantik bow). The beam was also increased by 60cm from 69.75ft (21.3m) to 71.75ft (21.9m). The increased length, coupled with relocation of the catapult allowed the incorporation of a double hangar on the *Prinz Eugen*, in lieu of the single hangar in *Hipper* and *Blücher*. A high-pressure steam plant was selected because, in principle, the technology promised to provide more efficient power than the lower pressure steam plants of the light cruisers. The steam turbine machinery would be lighter and smaller than diesel engines and produce less vibration. However, in practice the high-pressure steam plant never did provide the efficiencies anticipated, and also proved very prone to breakdowns. The plant was designed to produce 133,631shp, giving the ships a maximum speed of 32.5kts.

Prinz Eugen was laid down on 23 April 1936, launched on 22 August 1938 and completed on 1 August 1940. *Seydlitz* and *Lützow* were to be built to the *Prinz Eugen* dimensions and layout, and although neither was completed, both were launched before the start of the war. *Seydlitz* was laid down 29 December 1936 and launched on 29 January 1939, while *Lützow* was laid down on 2 August 1937 and launched on 1 July 1939. All three cruisers completed had the same armament of eight 8in guns in twin mounts, twelve 4.1in guns in twin mounts, twelve 37mm AA in twin mounts and eight 20mm AA single mounts. Each had four triple tube 21in torpedo mounts and three aircraft. The anti-aircraft fit was very heavy for the time, especially compared to the woeful AA fits of contemporary Royal Navy and US Navy cruisers. As the *Hipper* and *Blücher* were completing, naval observers in other countries could see the large size of the cruisers and their heavy armament, which raised doubts about the claimed adherence the 10,000-ton treaty limit. In reality, the ships exceeded treaty limitations by a huge 40 per cent. Although some questioned the veracity of Germany's bland assurances of compliance, in this period of appeasement no country was prepared to make it an issue. By then it was 1939 and Europe was about to erupt into war and the ships of the *Hipper* class were soon to be in action.

The late-war appearance of the ship is seen in this well-known view of *Prinz Eugen* interned at Copenhagen, Denmark, in April 1945.

Careers

If any member of the Admiral *Hipper* class has name recognition, it is clearly the *Prinz Eugen*. However, this fame is largely based on her association with the *Bismarck*, as opposed to her actual combat achievements. In fact, the *Admiral Hipper* was the only member of the class to achieve significant operational success in the Atlantic.

ADMIRAL HIPPER

On 29 April 1939 *Admiral Hipper* was completed but still required a very lengthy work up period. As the first unit to be completed, *Hipper* was the test bed for the design, and trials proved that the class had significant design problems with the straight bow, bridge arrangements and funnel fumes in the superstructure. Remedial work included the fitting of the raked *Atlantik* bow and a funnel cap. Along with *Scharnhorst* and *Gneisenau*, *Admiral Hipper* was dispatched on *Operation Nordmark*, a sweep for merchant shipping between Norway and the Shetland Islands, her first wartime sortie. The sweep was very short as no victims or opponents were found, but the cruiser suffered problems with her boilers and one of her turbines – the first example of what would prove to be the primary weakness of the class and particularly so in the case of *Hipper*.

In March 1940 *Hipper* prepared for her next action, *Operation Weserübung*, the German invasion of Norway. *Hipper* was the flag for Group 2, consisting of *Hipper* and four destroyers, which was transporting 1700 troops to occupy Trondheim. The force sortied on 6 April and the next day was joined by *Scharnhorst* and *Gneisenau*. The weather was poor as the force neared Norway and one of the German destroyers encountered a lone British destroyer, HMS *Glowworm*, which had been an escort for the battlecruiser *Renown* but was detached to search for one of her crewmen swept overboard in the poor weather. The German destroyer requested assistance and *Hipper* was sent to her aid. Shortly before 10:00am 8 April 1940 *Hipper* fired her guns in anger for the first time. The *Hipper* approached bow on, intentionally halving her fire in order to provide a minimum target for British torpedoes. The tactics were excellent as the first salvo of five British torpedoes passed *Hipper* on both sides. An early hit to *Glowworm*'s superstructure wrecked her wireless, but the destroyer proved very efficient in hiding in her smoke screen, leaving the *Hipper* to fire based on the destroyer's mast heads. *Glowworm* turned and launched her next salvo of five torpedoes but they were also avoided. When she came out of the smoke, *Glowworm* was so close that the German 20mm could range across the destroyer's bridge. With no torpedoes, only three 4.7in guns and taking on water, *Glowworm*'s captain, Lieutenant-Commander Roope, knew his ship was doomed but reversed course to ram the *Hipper* under the starboard anchor, creating a gash running all the way to the cruiser's torpedo mount amidship. However, the ramming was more of a glancing blow, rather than a puncture. As the destroyer fell away aft, the *Hipper*'s stern armament opened up but soon ceased firing when it became obvious that *Glowworm* was sinking.

Although the *Hipper* took on over 500 tons of water and her starboard torpedo mount was destroyed, she remained combat effective and was ordered to proceed to Trondheim to land her embarked troops. No significant resistance was encountered and *Hipper* and the destroyers anchored and disembarked their troops. On 10 April *Hipper* left Trondheim and set course for Germany to repair the damage from *Glowworm*, en route narrowly avoiding contact with a vastly superior British force. On 12 April *Hipper* joined *Scharnhorst* and *Gneisenau* and entered port that night. Repairs lasted into May and on the 8th the *Hipper* again went to sea to test her repairs in the Baltic.

On 4 June *Hipper*, *Scharnhorst*, *Gneisenau* and four destroyers sortied in *Operation Juno*, intended to relieve the allied pressure on Narvik and attack the British base at Harstad. The force had only sparse intelligence about allied naval forces, but reports soon suggested that the British were evacuating rather than reinforcing their positions. The force commander, Admiral Marschall, acting on his own initiative, chose to ignore his orders and shape a new plan to intercept the

ADMIRAL HIPPER CLASS KEY DATES

	Laid Down	Launched	Completed	Fate
Admiral Hipper	6 July 1935	6 February 1937	29 April 1939	Broken up 1948
Blücher	15 August 1935	8 June 1937	20 September 1939	Sunk 10 April 1940, Oslo Fjord
Prinz Eugen	23 April 1936	22 August 1938	1 August 1940	Capsized December 1947
Seydlitz	29 December 1936	19 January 1939	Never completed	Scuttled January 1945
Lützow	2 August 1937	1 July 1939	Never completed	Broken up 1960

Hipper at sea in company with *Scharnhorst* and *Gneisenau*, returning to Germany after the Norwegian operation in April 1940.

retreating British. On the morning of the 8th the force encountered two British ships and *Hipper* sank the armed trawler *Juniper*, while *Scharnhorst* and a destroyer sank the tanker *Oil Pioneer*. Later that morning *Hipper* found a more significant target: an empty troopship, the 19,840-ton *Orama*, which was sunk by the *Hipper*'s main guns. After this the *Hipper* and the destroyers were detached to do a sweep off Trondheim, while *Scharnhorst* and *Gneisenau* went north looking for victims, later sinking the carrier *Glorious* and two destroyers. *Hipper* became the sole heavy ship off Norway after both battleships returned to Germany, but the cruiser encountered more power plant problems, reducing maximum speed to 25kts to avoid putting more stress on the machinery. Even with her malfunctioning engines, *Hipper* was ordered to sweep the Arctic Ocean to intercept merchant traffic reported along the northern Scandinavian coast. This sweep lasted from 27 July until 6 August but only two small merchantmen were found, one of which was seized as a prize. *Hipper* returned to Germany for repairs to her engines on 11 August, the work lasting well into September.

On 24 September 1940 *Hipper* left on what was intended to be her first North Atlantic raid, but soon after departure the cruiser lost her starboard engine after that turbine's cooling pump broke down. *Hipper* had technicians flown into Norway to fix the pump, and on the 27th *Hipper* tried again, only for another engineering casualty to occur. A pipe burst, spraying the starboard turbine with lubricating oil and setting it on fire. The *Hipper* had to be brought to a dead stop in heavy seas to uncouple the engine and put out the fire to avoid complete destruction of the starboard turbine. After the engine was uncoupled, the raid was aborted and *Hipper* returned to Kiel for repairs, which were completed by 28 October. In November orders were issued for another commerce raid into the North Atlantic, timed to catch convoys anticipated by pattern analysis. In a departure from previous German heavy ship orders, the *Hipper*'s captain could attack convoys with weak escorts and was given a high degree of individual discretion. Oilers would be prepositioned at set refuelling points to keep the *Hipper* at sea.

The mission was named *Operation Nordseetour* and on 30 November *Hipper* made her second attempt to break into the North Atlantic, which she reached on 6 December. However, on the 10th the starboard shaft again had to be uncoupled because of turbine damage, reducing maximum speed to 25kts. Finally on the afternoon of 24 December contact was made with a convoy. Early on the 25th *Hipper* made a radar ranged torpedo attack, which was unsuccessful, but the British realised that the convoy was being tracked. Thereafter *Hipper* followed the convoy, intending to make a dawn attack for surprise as well as sufficient time to sink as many merchantmen as possible. The convoy was thought to be one of the weakly protected merchant convoys but what *Hipper* had really stumbled across was the heavily escorted troop convoy WS5A. A little after 6am *Hipper* closed to attack the convoy only to find a rude surprise awaiting her.

The first ship sighted was not a weak trawler or out-gunned destroyer but a 'County' class heavy cruiser, HMS *Berwick*, which along with the light cruisers *Bonaventure* and *Dunedin* and the carrier *Furious*, were escorting this high priority convoy. Luckily for *Hipper* the *Furious* was carrying crated aircraft and like *Glorious* in 1940 had no aircraft ready for combat operations. Nevertheless, *Hipper* wisely chose to break contact and a running duel occurred between the forward guns of *Berwick* and aft guns of *Hipper*, while the *Hipper*'s 105mm guns engaged the British light cruisers. The results were one sided in *Hipper*'s favour, as no hits were scored on the German cruiser, whereas *Hipper* hit *Berwick* four times with her 8in shells, knocking out X turret and causing flooding in the British cruiser. Rain squalls ended the engagement and *Hipper* broke clear of her pursuers. In addition to the four hits on *Berwick*, *Hipper* had damaged two merchant ships, one a troop-ship. After this narrow escape, facing malfunctioning machinery, ammunition expenditure and problematic reprovisioning, *Hipper* headed for Brest. After encountering the solitary 6000-ton cargo ship *Jumna*, which was quickly dispatched, *Hipper* arrived at Brest on 27 December 1940 with only one merchant ship to show for her month at sea.

On 1 February 1941 *Hipper* sortied for her third attempt to get at the convoys. This mission was designed to use the *Hipper* as a diversion to mask a concurrent raid by *Scharnhorst* and *Gneisenau* from Germany. In *Operation Wilmersdorf* the cruiser went south near the Azores to attack north-south convoys, but it was not until the 11th that *Hipper* found a straggler from one of the convoys, the small 1200-ton *Iceland*. After evacuating the merchant's crew the ship was sunk and *Hipper* again resumed the search for her main target, HG53. Multiple contacts were made by *Hipper*'s radar and the cruiser used the night hours to circle the convoy to form an appraisal of its size and possible escort strength. *Hipper* had not encountered HG53 but instead had found convoy SLS64, consisting of nineteen merchant ships with no escort. This was a perfect target but as the night wore on the sea state rose, which would hamper the *Hipper* during the day. It was decided to attack from the west at first light, and when the convoy was sighted at 05:15 men and officers alike were amazed to see that there was no opposing escort. At 06:18 *Hipper* opened fire, at which time the convoy commodore discovered the mortal threat and ordered the convoy to scatter.

Hipper ploughed into her victims, loosing all of her torpedoes and firing quickly to sink as many ships as possible before they became too separated. The sea state, rain squalls, fog, intentional smoke from fleeing steamers, smoke from burning victim's all slowed *Hipper*'s progress of destruction. With each minute that passed, the surviving merchant ships became further separated, making it progressively longer for *Hipper* to find the next target. By 06:45 *Hipper* had used two-thirds of her HE shells. There were still survivors slowing chugging away from the scene of carnage at 07:40 when *Hipper* broke off the action. Her massacre of the convoy had consumed almost all of her ammunition and she was down to a bare minimum to save in case of encountering opposition during her return to a friendly port. *Hipper* reported sinking thirteen ships totalling 75,000 tons, even though the actual tally was seven ships totalling 32,806 tons, *Hipper*'s massacre of SLS64 was the most successful convoy interception ever executed by any single German heavy surface ship. *Hipper* triumphantly docked at Brest on 14 February, leaving again on 15 March for Germany for a refit, taking the Arctic circle route and making Kiel on the 28th.

Although *Hipper* went back to Trondheim in March, no major operation was scheduled until 2 July 1942 when *Hipper* took part in *Operation Rösselsprung*, an attack on Russian convoy PQ17. *Tirpitz*, *Scheer*, *Hipper* and four destroyers were deployed for this task. Admiral Dudley Pound knew that the heavy German force was at sea and withdrew the convoy's heavy support and ordered the convoy to scatter, resulting in the wholesale destruction of the merchant ships by U-boats and aircraft. Aware that their heavy ships were being tracked, German naval command termi-

SUMMARY OF SHIPS SUNK BY *ADMIRAL HIPPER*

Date	Name	Type	Displacement
6 April 1940	HMS *Glowworm*	destroyer	1350 tons
8 June 1940	HMS *Juniper*	armed trawler	545 tons
8 June 1940	*Orama*	troopship	19,840 tons
August 1940	*Ester Thorden* (seized)	cargo	1940 tons
25 December 1940	*Jumna*	cargo	6078 tons
11 February 1941	*Iceland*	cargo	1236 tons
12 February 1941	*Borgestad*	cargo	3924 tons
12 February 1941	*Derrynane*	cargo	4896 tons
12 February 1941	*Ostwestry Grange*	cargo	4684 tons
12 February 1941	*Perseus*	cargo	5172 tons
12 February 1941	*Shrewsbury*	cargo	4542 tons
12 February 1941	*Warlaby*	cargo	4876 tons
12 February 1941	*Westbury*	cargo	4712 tons
31 December 1942	HMS *Bramble*	minesweeper	815 tons
31 December 1942	HMS *Achates*	destroyer	1340 tons

Hipper at anchor in Brest, France, in March 1941 after her highly successful attack on convoy SLS64 in which seven ships were sunk. This was the greatest single convoy loss to a German surface raider of the war.

nated the operation late on the 5th and the ships reached port the following day. Captain Meisel of *Hipper* requested to be allowed to go after the surviving ships of the now scattered convoy but was denied. *Operation Zarin* was undertaken by *Hipper* and four destroyers starting on 24 September with the mission to lay mines off the coast of Novaya Zemlya. For this novel task *Hipper* carried 96 mines, which were deployed late on the 26th. *Hipper* intercepted signals from a Soviet icebreaker but Captain Meisel's request to search out the ship was denied and *Hipper* returned to Norway the following day.

Admiral Hipper was the flagship of a German force, also including the *panzerschiffe Lützow* and six destroyers, which left Norway on 30 December 1942 for an attack on convoy JW51B, code-named *Operation Regenbogen*. The Battle of the Barents Sea began when *Hipper* picked up the convoy and notified *Lützow* to attack from the south, while *Hipper* circled to the north with three destroyers to drive the convoy into the 11in guns of *Lützow*. Close convoy support consisted of four destroyers. *Hipper* was engaging the destroyer *Achates* when attacked by two others, *Onslow* and *Orwell*. Four 8in shells hit *Onslow* causing serious damage while *Hipper*'s 105mm secondary guns engaged *Orwell*. Both destroyers steered away concealed by their smoke screens, as well as hiding in snow squalls. By now the cruisers HMS *Sheffield* and *Jamaica* were only 15 miles away and closing quickly. *Hipper* then came across the minesweeper *Bramble*, which was soon left blazing. *Hipper* encountered *Achates* a second time and set her on fire with her first salvo. The other three British destroyers, which had been to the south to ward off *Lützow*, now came north to assist *Achates*. At 11:30 *Hipper* was surrounded by shell splashes from *Sheffield* and *Jamaica*. Visibility had been much worse to the north than the south and the British cruisers had closed to 11,000yds before firing on the *Hipper*, whose concentration had been fixed on the four British destroyers to the south. Furthermore, *Hipper*'s radar had been disabled from the concussion of her own guns, so it took *Hipper* three minutes to sight her new assailants and in the meantime she was holed by a 6in shell below the armour belt which exploded in a fuel bunker. It was not until 11:34 that *Hipper* replied to the fire of the light cruisers. *Hipper* received two more hits, one to the hull and one to the hangar, both of which caused fires. Kummetz ordered the convoy attack broken off and raced west to get away from the British cruisers. *Sheffield* and *Jamaica* chased the *Hipper* and *Lützow* until around 14:00 when the pursuit was halted. During this period *Achates* finally sank from the damages inflicted by *Hipper*. But all was not well on the German cruiser: flooding caused by the first hit cost the *Hipper* the boilers in number three room, and then water started flooding the number two boiler room, which was shut down by 17:30. *Hipper* was reduced to a very slow speed and was lucky that the British had broken off the chase five hours earlier. She made the safety of Norway early on 1 January 1943.

Hitler had anticipated a major victory from *Operation Regenbogen* and been asking for updates. The first news came in from the BBC, which portrayed the action as a handful of destroyers chasing away a heavy cruiser, a pocket battleship and a hoard of destroyers. Hitler flew into an uncontrolled rage and ordered that all the heavy ships should be scrapped. This was never carried out, but from this point *Hipper* and most of the other remaining heavy German surface units were limited to supporting the army in the Baltic. *Hipper*

The wreck of the *Admiral Hipper* after removal from drydock at Kiel to Heikendorf Bay, late in 1945.

was not repaired after the Battle of Barents Sea but was placed immediately into reserve with just a skeleton crew. Finally in March 1944 it was decided to recommission the ship to provide fire support on the fast deteriorating Eastern Front. Original plans were to have *Hipper* operational by November 1944, but this was not met. On 29 January 1945 she was ordered west and on her way to Kiel passed the sinking liner *Wilhelm Gustloff*. With *Hipper*'s crippled state, her captain kept her on course without stopping to pick up survivors already on life rafts. She arrived on 2 February and was still under repair on 3 May when she was seriously hit in the last RAF bomber raid. After the war the hulk was broken up.

Blücher on initial trials in the Baltic, shortly after commissioning in September 1939. Note that the admiral's bridge is completely open to the elements.

BLÜCHER

The operational career of the second member of the class was extraordinarily short and her fate exhibits the folly of committing a ship to combat before it is completely worked up. Commissioned on 20 September 1939, trials for *Blücher* were delayed by additional work to fit the *Atlantik* bow and raked funnel cap, so it was not until 27 November that the ship left for trials in the Baltic. The very severe winter then hampered trials so by March 1940 *Blücher* has spent only 19 days at sea and the crew had received only minimal training. Nonetheless, *Blücher* was included in *Operation Weserübung*, the invasion of Norway. She was tasked with transporting troops to the closest but toughest target, Oslo. Rear Admiral Kummetz was the Group commander, flying his flag on *Blücher* (this same admiral later flew his flag from *Hipper* in the Battle of Barents Sea). *Blücher* still had a high proportion of practice ammunition in her magazine and scheduling was so tight that this was not removed. Instead war rounds were added on top of the practice rounds. When the army troops embarked, they brought their own ammunition, and with no space in the magazines, this ammunition was stored on the main deck and in the hangar. On 8 April *Blücher*, followed by *Lützow* and *Emden*, sailed for Oslo. Later that night *Blücher* entered the fjord leading to Oslo. She swept past a guard boat and was then illuminated by searchlights and a warning shot fired. The force continued their journey up the fjord and reached the narrows shortly before 05:00 on the 9th. Suddenly a searchlight again illuminated the new cruiser. Forty minutes later two 1891 model Krupp 280mm coastal defence guns opened fire on *Blücher*. At the range of 2000yds, it was hard to miss even with this ancient ordnance. The first round struck the flak control platform and smoke filled the tower bridge, The location of the Norwegian fire could not be identified so many guns opened wild, untargeted fire. Another 280mm shell slammed into the hangar, which still held her inflammable aircraft as well as army ammunition. At this time a 150mm battery less than a half mile from *Blücher* opened up and quickly scored twenty hits. Amidship was a mass of flame and, with the rudder jammed, the ship had to be manoeuvred with engines until a jury rig rudder was brought into operation. At this time she took two torpedo hits from a land-based torpedo battery. She still steamed up the fjord at 15 knots but *Lützow* and *Emden* did not follow. The torpedoes stuck near the turbine rooms and power systems started shutting down. Neither the admiral, nor the officers of *Blücher* recognised how seriously the ship was damaged. The turbine for the centreline shaft stopped, and finally the turbines for the outboard shafts also quit, leaving the *Blücher* with no power. The ship dropped the starboard anchor but did not beach herself when she had the momentum to do so. As the untrained damage control parties fought the fires, they were further hampered by army ammunition and grenades cooking off. Then the fire reached a 105mm shell magazine and the resulting explosion ruptured the bunkers and ignited the fuel oil. The captain finally realised that his new command was doomed and ordered the ship abandoned at 07:00; half an hour later *Blücher* rolled over and sank bow first. Since there was an island only 350 yards distant, there were many survivors, including Admiral Kummetz.

Blücher at anchor in Kiel harbour, January 1940. Heavy ice problems immobilised fleet, delaying the ship's work-up. By this time the admiral's bridge has been closed in

PRINZ EUGEN

There were two significant events which have immortalised the *Prinz Eugen*: the sortie with the *Bismarck*, and the 'Channel Dash'.

Completed on 1 August 1940, *Prinz Eugen* spent the balance of the year in trials or making adjustments at the yard. In early 1941 it was more of the same but in the spring the cruiser began joint training with *Bismarck* in preparation for their sortie, *Operation Rheinübung*, an Atlantic raid that kicked off on 19 May 1941. As the ships left port to navigate the narrows between Denmark and Sweden, they had been spotted and reported to the British so by the morning of 21 May when the pair arrived in Norway the British had a full search under way to locate them. They left that night with *Bismarck* in the lead and on the 23rd were skirting the ice pack of Greenland when detected by British cruisers. *Bismarck* disabled her forward radar by the concussion of firing at HMS *Norfolk* so *Prinz Eugen* was ordered to take point, so her radar could be used to see what was ahead. At 04:00 on the 24th *Prinz Eugen* detected engine noise coming from the east towards the German ships. Shortly thereafter it was determined that there were two ships in company rapidly approaching. As daylight broke the trailing cruisers were seen as well as the new pair in the distance, which initially were thought to be another two cruisers. The pair was HMS *Hood* and HMS *Prince of Wales*, which opened fire at 05:53. Fire was directed at *Prinz Eugen* because she was the lead ship and thought to be *Bismarck*. Two minutes later *Prinz Eugen* fired at *Hood* at 21,000yds. The first salvo of *Hood* was well aimed and bracketed the cruiser. *Prinz Eugen* bracketed *Hood* in return and a shell from her third salvo struck the battlecruiser's shelter deck and started a huge fire between the funnels and mainmast. After this, fire was shifted to *Prince of Wales* at 05:59 to keep her occupied while *Bismarck* continued to aim at *Hood*. The first salvo from *Prinz Eugen* had two hits aft on the British battleship. The fifth salvo of *Bismarck* detonated the aft magazine of *Hood*, which broke in two and quickly sank. *Prinz Eugen* continued firing at *Prince of Wales* and scored at least two more hit before the British battleship broke off the engagement at 06:09 behind a smoke screen.

Of the four 8in shell hits on *Prince of Wales*, because of a faulty fuse design only one shell exploded. *Prinz Eugen* was undamaged but *Bismarck* had been hit, the most serious of which had opened the bow fuel bunker. This single hit would have significant consequences because the *Bismarck* lost fuel and thus range, went down by the bow, reducing maximum speed by two knots, and trailed an oil slick. Later that day Admiral Lutjens ordered the *Prinz Eugen* to break away to continue the raid, while *Bismarck* would turn on their shadowers and then make for France for repairs. The separation was successful and the *Prinz Eugen* proceeded, looking to duplicate the performance of *Hipper* a few months earlier. *Prinz Eugen* needed fuel, which was not obtained until the 26th. The cruiser briefly loitered on the convoy routes, when she received news of the loss of *Bismarck*. By now *Prinz Eugen* started encountering machinery problems, as *Hipper* had done, although not to the same extent. Nevertheless, an escalating series of plant problems reduced the cruiser's speed to

Admiral Lütjens leaving the *Prinz Eugen* after a visit to the ship at Gotenhafen, May 1941. She was about to sail with *Bismarck* for *Operation Rheinübung*, under Lütjens' overall command.

Prinz Eugen's AA guns in action during the Channel Dash, 12 February 1942.

28kts, and on 31 May she turned for Brest, arriving on 1 June.

After the sortie the British snapped up the network of supply oilers, which were a key component of surface ships raids. As a result, the *Prinz Eugen*, along with *Scharnhorst* and *Gneisenau*, spent the rest of 1941 as a target for the RAF at Brest, where one would be hit from time to time. Clearly, remaining so close to British air bases was untenable and the risk would only increase since the United States had entered the war. In February 1942 Hitler, who wanted the ships in Norway, ordered them to return to Germany via the English Channel. *Operation Cerberus*, or the Channel Dash, started on the evening of 11 February 1942. The force was already in the Channel before they were spotted on the morning of the 12th. *Prinz Eugen* came under fire by Dover shore batteries around 13:20 as she moved through the narrowest part of the Channel. After 15 minutes in which the cruiser was not hit, she was out of range. Then the British launched various attacks. The escorting destroyers broke up an attack by MTBs and destroyers and at 13:43 six Swordfish came in and *Prinz Eugen* claimed three of them shot down. For the next hour there were occasional light air attacks and the cruiser claimed a two-engined bomber. *Scharnhorst* hit a mine at 15:30 so *Prinz Eugen* and *Gneisenau* continued on, leaving *Scharnhorst* behind. At 16:43 a cruiser and three destroyers approached and in an inconclusive eleven-minute exchange one British destroyer was damaged. After another series of uncoordinated air attacks, night fell but the sea state rose reducing the cruiser to 31kts. Although close to design maximum speed the *Gneisenau* could maintain 32kts and left the cruiser behind. However, there were to be no more attacks and *Prinz Eugen* reached Germany on the morning of 13 February. There was no damage sustained by the cruiser other than crew casualties caused by strafing. On February 19 the cruiser left for Norway in company with *Scheer*.

On 22 February the pair arrived at Grimstadfjord from where *Prinz Eugen* had departed with *Bismarck* almost exactly nine months earlier. In those nine months German surface ships had changed roles from predators to prey. On 23 February south of Trondheim the submarine HMS *Trident* spotted the German force with *Scheer* in the lead and fired a spread of torpedoes. One struck *Prinz Eugen* on her stern and destroyed her rudders and caused the extreme stern to collapse at an angle into the sea like a ramp. The cruiser came to a stop in broad daylight to make temporary repairs. Finally, steering by engines, she could make ten knots and limped into Trondheim that night. Jury rudders had to be built in Germany and sent to Trondheim. Fitting the jury rudders took until 9 May and, under the code-name *Operation Zauberflöte*, *Prinz Eugen* departed for

Germany on 16 May bound for full repairs. On the 17th the *Prinz Eugen* was attacked by the RAF in torpedo and bombing attacks, but *Prinz Eugen* was not hit and the British lost four aircraft. The ship arrived at Kiel on the 18th and repairs and a refit took until 27 October, when the *Prinz Eugen* left for the Baltic for trials. *Prinz Eugen* never returned to Norway and the cruiser was fated to spend the rest of the war in the Baltic.

After the Battle of Barents Sea all of the heavy ships were aid up as per Hitler's orders, except that *Prinz Eugen* continued to provide training, along with the *Emden*. In June 1944 *Prinz Eugen* was ordered to the Gulf of Finland to provide fire support for the hard-pressed Finns. Nothing was accomplished and the cruiser returned to Gotenhafen at the end of the month. In July the situation of the Wehrmacht in the Baltic States reached a crisis and *Prinz Eugen* was ordered to provide support in the Gulf of Riga with the ship's Arados providing observation. This was conducted on 19 July and among other fire support missions, the cruiser silenced Red Army artillery, which had been taking pot shots at her. She returned to Gotenhafen the 21st and when the Red Army launched another offensive the *Prinz Eugen* went back to support the Wehrmacht. As fall progressed, the German army was folding under Soviet pressure and the cruiser's guns were in constant demand. On 15 October *Prinz Eugen* was just reaching Gotenhafen at night when *Leipzig* was leaving. It was foggy and the naval staff had not coordinated the movement of the two cruisers, which collided. The heavy cruiser drove her raked bow deeply into the port side hull of *Leipzig* amidships, remaining locked together until late the following day. Repairs took until 7 November and *Prinz Eugen* went back to alternating with *Scheer* in providing the army fire support. Her guns were worn out and in December the cruiser went in for a refit for the next six weeks. By late January the Red Army had cut off the cruiser's old base of Gotenhafen but she continued to use the port as long as there was ammunition stored there. By now there were few 8in rounds to be found and the *Scheer* took up the fire support duties. The cruiser was hit by Soviet rocket fire on 30 March and expended her last 40 rounds of 8in shells on 4 April. With no further supplies of ammunition *Prinz Eugen* retreated to Copenhagen on 20 April, where she remained until Germany surrendered.

Prinz Eugen became a prize of the United States. She entered service under the US flag on 5 January 1946, designated *IX-300*. She then steamed to Boston with an American crew for a detailed examination. However, her final destination was Bikini Atoll in the South Pacific as a target of an A-bomb test. Test Able was conducted on 1 July 1946 with the nuclear bomb fused for air burst. The cruiser was anchored about a mile from the centre and received little damage. However, the second test was for an underwater burst. Test Baker buckled the hull's plating. The *Prinz Eugen* still survived the summer's testing but was radioactive so no crew was kept on board. On December 21, after silently taking in water through loose fittings for months, the cruiser developed a list and was beached, but the next day she capsized. The wreck of the *Prinz Eugen* can still be found on Kwajalein Island with her stern out of water and her bow 100 feet below the surface.

Following torpedo damage, the truncated stern of *Prinz Eugen* shows the jury rudders rigged for the voyage back to Germany for permanent repairs, May 1942.

Seydlitz under construction, early in 1941, at Deschimag, Bremen. Much of the structural work is complete and the main armament has been mounted, but not a lot more was done before the decision was taken in May 1942 to convert the ship to an aircraft carrier.

SEYDLITZ/WESER

The fourth unit of the class was *Seydlitz*. Laid down on 29 December 1936 and launched on 1 January 1939, the cruiser was never completed. After the war started that September, work on the cruiser slowed as material and manpower constraints made themselves felt. However, by May 1942 *Seydlitz* was very close to completion, missing only the cranes, catapult, masts and light AA. By this time it was abundantly clear to the German command that their failure to provide carrier-based aviation had been an extraordinarily large mistake. Like Japan on the other side of the world, the German navy decided to convert the cruiser into an aircraft carrier to be named the *Weser*. For the next year the *Seydlitz* was slowly reduced, as the turrets and superstructure were removed, leaving only the hull and funnel. She was moved to Königsberg in 1944 but in December was reclassified as a hulk, which was scuttled on 29 January 1945 to prevent her from falling into Soviet hands.

LÜTZOW/PROJECT 53

The fifth unit of the class was *Lützow*, which was laid down on 2 August 1937 and launched on 1 July 1939. Rather than expend more effort to complete the cruiser, *Lützow* was transferred to the Soviet Union as part of the agreement between the two countries in August 1939. The actual purchase was on 11 February 1940. By this time A and D turrets were in place with guns only in A turret and the lower superstructure had been constructed. When towed to Leningrad on 15 April, Germany sent 70 technicians under a rear admiral to supervise and assist completion of the cruiser by the Soviets. As 1941 dawned, parts deliveries were delayed and then the number of German technicians started diminishing. In spring the German rear admiral excused himself from Leningrad by stating that he needed urgent medical treatment in Germany; the last technician bolted just before Germany's invasion of Russia. In Russia the *Lützow* first became Project 53 and then was given the name *Petropavlovsk*. When Germany forces crossed the border *Petropavlovsk* was 70 per cent complete. At this time D turret had its guns as well as some 37mm AA guns. On 15 August the *Petropavlovsk* was commissioned in her incomplete state. On 7 September 1941 the former *Lützow* went into action against her former owners as a floating battery, firing at German troops closing Leningrad. In the next six days she fired almost 700 8in shells. On 17 September German counter battery fire knocked out her electrical generator and the ship, including the turrets, lost power, as well as suffering over 50 hits. The ship was towed to Leningrad's Baltic yard in September 1942 and repaired but one of the 8in guns remained out of service. The ship was renamed *Tallin* and in January 1944 went into action again, providing 31 fire support missions and expending over 1000 8in rounds as the Red Army burst from Leningrad in a winter offensive. The Soviets decided not to complete the cruiser but she was used as an accommodation ship until 1960 when she was scrapped.

The incomplete *Lützow* under tow to Russia, 15 April 1940. Turret Anton and its guns have been mounted and the turret, but not the guns for Dora were also in place.

Model Products

By their very nature, plastic models of cruisers have less 'crowd appeal' than battleship or aircraft carrier kits and when it came to the *Hipper* class cruisers, manufacturers chose the more famous *Prinz Eugen* over the work-a-day *Hipper*. The first plastic kits of *Prinz Eugen* and *Hipper* made their appearances in a series of 1:1200 scale plastic first in the United Kingdom under the Eaglewall brand and then subsequently in the US under the Pyro label in the early 1960s. It was not until the late 1960s that a larger kit in the form of the Revell 1:720 scale *Prinz Eugen* appeared. It was always *Prinz Eugen* that gained the spotlight. Airfix only produced the *Prinz Eugen* and although Heller produced both kits, the *Prinz Eugen* was produced in far greater quantities than their low production *Hipper*. When Tamiya finally got round to producing a 1:700 scale model of the class, their choice was again *Prinz Eugen*. The shameful neglect of poor over-looked *Admiral Hipper* is finally coming to an end courtesy of Trumpeter Models from China. As this is being written, the first of Trumpeter's models of the class has been released in the form of the 1:350 scale 1945 fit for *Prinz Eugen*. Trumpeter has announced production of a 1941 fit for *Admiral Hipper* in 1:350 scale and kits of the *Prinz Eugen* in 1942 and 1945 fits. Quite often Trumpeter will release the 1:350 scale kit of a subject and then follow up with 1:700 scale versions. One can only hope that the 1:350 scale *Hipper* will be followed with 1:700 versions, and perhaps a *Blücher* as well.

Collectors' 1:1250 Scale

NAVIS/NEPTUN *ADMIRAL HIPPER* CLASS BASIC SERIES

1:1250 Scale

To call these models basic is really a misnomer, as they are the best of their scale in the world, except for the same models finished to a higher level by the same manufacturer. This German firm is the most prominent European manufacturer of metal models of warships. Neptun is the brand name used for models of World War Two subjects. Neptun actually produces four different versions of *Hipper* class cruisers in the standard series: *Admiral Hipper* 1940, *Blücher* 1940, and *Prinz Eugen* in 1941 and 1945 fits. The details on these small models are outstanding and are only enhanced by the excellent and well-executed paint scheme. In addition to the overall grey, the models have accurate aluminum coloured stack caps, a black boot top and funnel interior, and brown boat tops.

Samples: **Courtesy of Navis/Neptun** and **Morning Sunshine Models** www.navis-neptun.de and www.collectableships.com

NAVIS/NEPTUN ***ADMIRAL HIPPER*** CLASS CAMOUFLAGED SERIES

1:1250 Scale

There are actually three different levels of camouflage detail, each at a correspondingly higher price. As an example the 1941 fit for *Prinz Eugen* has the standard all-grey version listed as model 1030, while the first level of camouflage has the Baltic black and white hull stripes and carmine turret crowns and is listed as T1030. The next step up includes the detail found with T1030 but also includes a painted deck, bow swastika markings and flag on the ensign staff and is designated model T1030S. The highest level of finish includes everything with the T1030S but also includes rigging, base with name plate and clear protective cover and is designated T1030V. Shown here is a photograph of the *Hipper* T1032 and the *Prinz Eugen* T1030 and T1030S versions.

■ Samples: **Courtesy of Navis/Neptun** and **Morning Sunshine Models** www.navis-neptun.de and www.collectableships.com

Mid-size Scales 1:600 to 1:720 Scale

The models in this scale range are by far the most popular and have become the battle ground among injected plastic and resin model manufacturers. The *Prinz Eugen* has always been the model produced, with very few exceptions – only the German firm of H-P models produced specific resin kits of *Admiral Hipper*, *Blücher* and *Prinz Eugen*.

REVELL ***PRINZ EUGEN***

1:720 Scale

The first model kit of any of the *Hipper* class cruisers was of course of the scene-stealing *Prinz Eugen*. First produced in the late 1960s by Revell, this 40-year-old kit is still available in a number of guises. Shown here is the current release of the kit with the latest Revell packaging, although inside the box is the same model you could have purchased four decades ago. Comparing the Revell *Prinz Eugen* with the Tamiya 1:700 scale *Prinz Eugen* highlights how much standards have changed. The

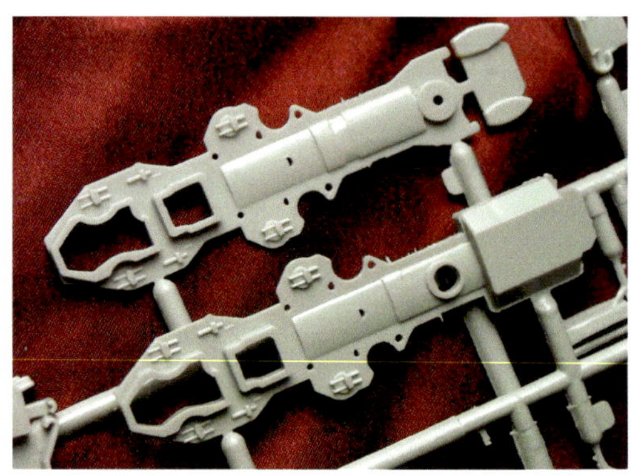

20mm, 37mm and torpedo mounts that are moulded into the deck are really a throwback to the blobs for detail found in the original injected plastic kit from Revell in 1952. The moulded on detail is truly appalling and cartoon-like; even the main gun turrets appear more like circus tents than the actual shape. Hull portholes are huge and deck detail is simplified. However, if price is your prime consideration, Revell still delivers a kit at a significantly lower price than the competition.

■ Sample: **Courtesy of Freetime Hobbies** www.freetimehobbies.com

REVELL ***BLÜCHER*** 1:720 Scale

I really expected that the Revell *Blücher* would be merely their *Prinz Eugen* with different box art. I was wrong: there is a difference between the two kits, but not reflecting the important fact that *Prinz Eugen* was fifteen feet longer than *Blücher*. The difference only amounts to one part but that one part changes the ship's profile and is one part more than I expected. That part is the hangar deck, which reverses the catapult position. Although this single change may seem somewhat lame, all credit to Revell for at least trying to present one of the differences between the sister-ships in this early kit.

■ Sample: **Courtesy of Freetime Hobbies**
www.freetimehobbies.com

MATCHBOX ***ADMIRAL HIPPER*** 1:720 Scale

In the early 1970s the Japanese consortium of Tamiya, Hasegawa, Aoshima and Fujimi popularised 1:700 scale waterline models as the world's standard for a mid-size kit. Nevertheless, a member of the *Hipper* class would not be produced by one of the Japanese firms for another 30 years. Into this void stepped the British firm of Matchbox. Only Matchbox took on the Japanese consortium by producing their own original mouldings for 1:700 scale kits. Sometimes Matchbox produced a competing kit against an established Japanese model, such as the Matchbox *Duke of York* version of a KGV class battleship, but more often than not Matchbox picked a subject not released by one of the Japanese manufacturers, such as HMS *Exeter* or USS *Indianapolis*. Although the Matchbox kits had some initial success, the company did not make a breakthrough against the Japanese competitors. In 1991 the *Admiral Hipper* was released under the Matchbox logo but something was amiss in that this kit was in 1:720 scale not the traditional 1:700 Matchbox scale. How odd! At least it was odd until you opened the box and saw the parts. A quick look at the side of the box confirmed the truth. There it was: © 1991 by Revell AG. In a Rope-A-Dope move, Revell of Germany had pulled out the old Revell USA trick of repackaging an old kit under new box art but had pushed the process a step further. Not only was there new box art but, to further bamboozle the modeller, Revell had stuck the Matchbox label on the box. The kit is not a *Hipper*: it is exactly the same as the original 1960s Revell USA *Prinz Eugen*.

■ Sample: **Author's Collection**

AIRFIX *PRINZ EUGEN* 1:600 Scale

The earliest Airfix kits in 1:600 scale were mainly British warship subjects, followed by German ships sunk by the Royal Navy, including *Bismarck*, *Scharnhorst* and *Graf Spee*. However, the *Prinz Eugen* is a notable exception to the trend, since she was not sunk, but was probably included because of her association with *Bismarck*. Airfix kits tended to increase in quality over time and the *Prinz Eugen* is a later release. Seen here is the Airfix kit as released in the US under the MPC label but it is the same kit as appeared in Airfix boxes. The bottom line is the Airfix *Prinz Eugen* is a good kit and was a tremendous leap in detail over the Revell 1:720 scale kit. On the plus side are the overall lines, nice superstructure detail and inclusion of the correct torpedo mounts with enclosed crew positions. However, it certainly is not

a perfect product as it does not have the stern anchor position on the port hull aft, and the external degaussing cable is overscale, but the hull does capture the *Prinz Eugen* profile. From the box art the kit initially appears as the fit for May 1941 with the Baltic stripe camouflage overpainted in Norway. However, the presence of 20mm *vierlings* on the model negates this fit, as this ordnance was not added to *Prinz Eugen* until December 1941. Also the May 1941 *Prinz Eugen* did not have the spherical protective covers on the forward

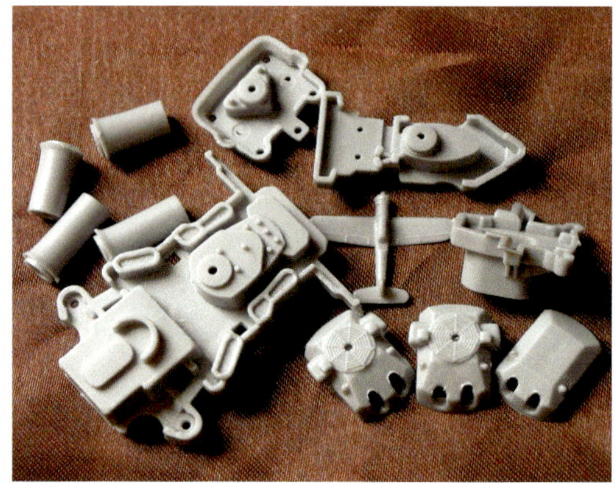

HA directors as depicted in the kit. To further complicate matters the *vierling* fit is wrong. Airfix provides five of the quadruple 20mm mounts – one on the tower superstructure platform, one each on Bruno and Caesar turret crowns and two for the funnel searchlight platform. *Prinz Eugen* never had this configuration, as the *vierlings* were added in the following order: December 1941 one each to Bruno and Caesar crowns with one on forecastle and one on quarterdeck; January 1942 a *vierling* replaces searchlight on tower platform; and May 1942 two searchlights on funnel platform replaced by *vierlings*. Not only is the fit wrong but also the 20mm and 37mm guns are too large and rather crude in detail. However, what was botched by Airfix of the UK is fixed by White Ensign Models of the UK with 1:600 scale photo-etch sets. Not for the inexperienced, WEM PE623 provides quadruple as well as single 20mm mounts curing the *vierling* crisis and set PE633 provides 1:600 scale ship specific parts to further improve the Airfix *Prinz Eugen*.

Sample: **Courtesy of Felix Bustelo**

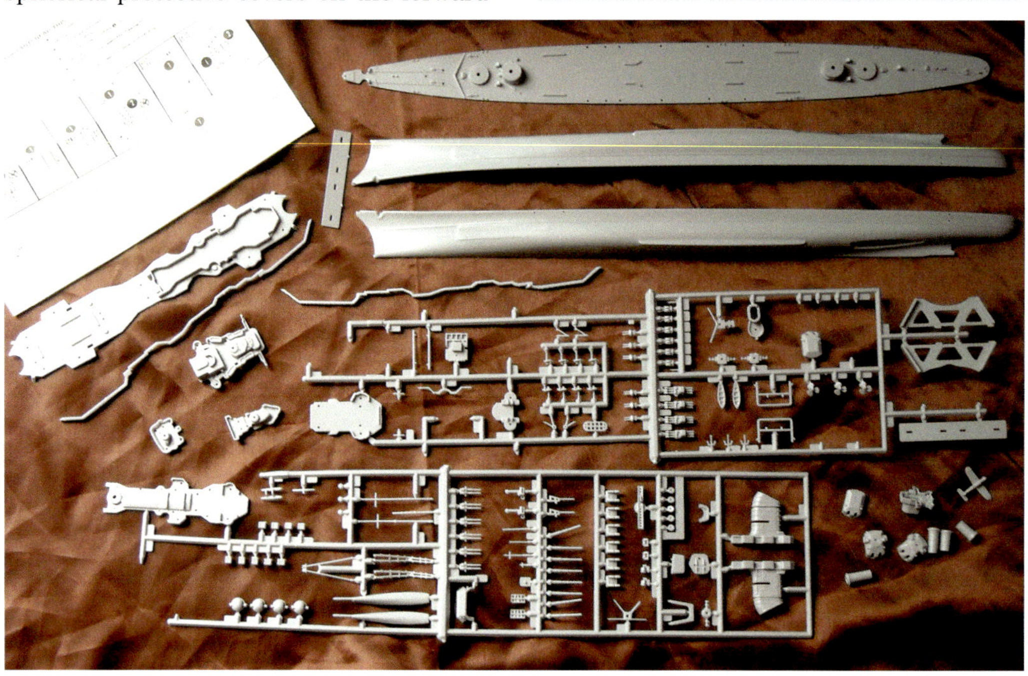

TAMIYA *PRINZ EUGEN* — 1:700 Scale

Released in 2002 the Tamiya *Prinz Eugen* is definitely the best 1:700 scale plastic kit of the class available at this time, but with two different versions of *Prinz Eugen* in the offing from Trumpeter, Tamiya may loose the title of best of scale in plastic. The box art shows the familiar Baltic stripe design with red turret crowns against a backdrop of ice covered mountains. Its positives far outweigh its negatives. For one thing Tamiya designers clearly researched their topic and realised that the *Prinz Eugen* of *Rheinübung* (May 1941) differed from the 1942 *Prinz Eugen*. Tamiya provides alternate parts for the early *Prinz Eugen* with no *vierling*s and searchlights still in place, and optional parts for the 1942 *Prinz Eugen*, either for *Operation Cerberus* early in 1942 or after she arrived in Germany. The primary difference is the *vierling*s replacing searchlights and the additional turret crown and deck *vierling*s. Unlike Airfix, Tamiya provides forecastle and quarterdeck *vierling*s. If you are modelling the *Rheinübung* version, no *vierling*s are used; if it is the *Prinz Eugen* of *Cerberus* in February 1942 five *vierling* mounts are used (on turret crowns, tower searchlight platform, forecastle and quarterdeck) but searchlights are still on the funnel platform; for May 1942 you replace the funnel platform searchlights with the optional *vierlings* provided. Hull and superstructure detail is very good but the main deck detail is a little sparse. Tamiya missed in a couple of areas. In conformance with the box art, the kit depicts the *Rheinübung* ship with the spherical covers that were not added until *Prinz Eugen* reached Brest. A more significant error comes in the form of the torpedo mounts, which depict the open crew position found on *Hipper* or *Blücher*, not the enclosed crew positions of *Prinz Eugen*.

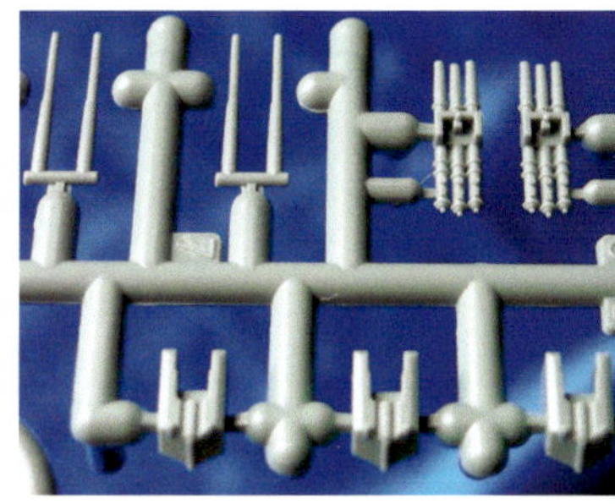

Sample: **Courtesy of Freetime Hobbies**
www.freetimehobbies.com

HI MOLD *PRINZ EUGEN* — 1:700 Scale

If you want a good balance between price and fidelity, the Tamiya *Prinz Eugen* is a very good option, but if you want the positively best 1:700 scale *Prinz Eugen* kit available, than your choice should be the Hi Mold *Prinz Eugen*. At the top of the line of Pit Road kits were the best kits this company had to offer, released under the Hi Mold logo. The resin parts were of exceptional quality but the kits were very expensive. Hi Mold released their version of *Prinz Eugen* as HM029. If you can find the kit, the Hi Mold *Prinz Eugen* will cost about four times as much as the Tamiya *Prinz Eugen*, but it is spot on for the *Operation Rheinübung Prinz Eugen*. Finally here is a

manufacturer that recreated the right fittings and right appearance for the raid with *Bismarck*. There are open HA directors on the forward HA positions, unlike the spherical covering provided by Tamiya, Airfix and others. The kit has the right AA and searchlight fittings for the raid. Resin with smaller parts in white metal, hull and superstructure detail is excellent. However, main deck detail is only on par with that of the Tamiya kit and is therefore disappointing considering the price you will pay to get this kit. In spite of that high price, no photo-etch is included, so you really must dig a little bit deeper to purchase photo-etch because this kit is too good to be short-changed on that final detail.

■ Sample: **Courtesy of David Lilly**

1:400 to 1:350 Scale

When it comes to *Admiral Hipper* class kits in larger scales, to date there has been a very limited selection. Iron Shipwright produced a $300+ resin and brass version, while Heller issued 1:400 scale versions of *Prinz Eugen* and *Admiral Hipper*, although the *Hipper* is by far the rarer of the two. This situation is dramatically changing as this title goes to press. Trumpeter has just released their first 1:350 scale kit on the class, *Prinz Eugen* 1945 and by the end of 2010 a 1:350 scale *Admiral Hipper* will be released.

HELLER *PRINZ EUGEN* 1:400 Scale

This has been the first choice for those modellers wanting a larger scale model of *Prinz Eugen*. This is one of the later Heller kits and comes with the hull and five sprues of parts. The kit is typical Heller with good hull lines, including degaussing cable. The deck has some problems with raised deck lines and lack of a breakwater. The kit comes with plastic railing, which may have been hi-tech in 1980 but is obsolete now. Don't use it: go with brass photo-etch instead. In spite of the box art, the Heller *Prinz Eugen* does not have the right fit for any time period, as it comes with AA guns on Bruno turret, Caesar turret and the tower searchlight platform and no *vierling* for forecastle, quarterdeck or funnel platform. Of course the forward HA towers have their spherical covers. Currently out of production, the Heller *Prinz Eugen* has previously commanded high prices at auction sites and the significantly rarer Heller *Hipper* even higher prices. With the appearance of the far superior Trumpeter 1:350 scale *Prinz Eugen* and upcoming Trumpeter *Hipper*, the auction prices on the Heller pair should drop significantly.

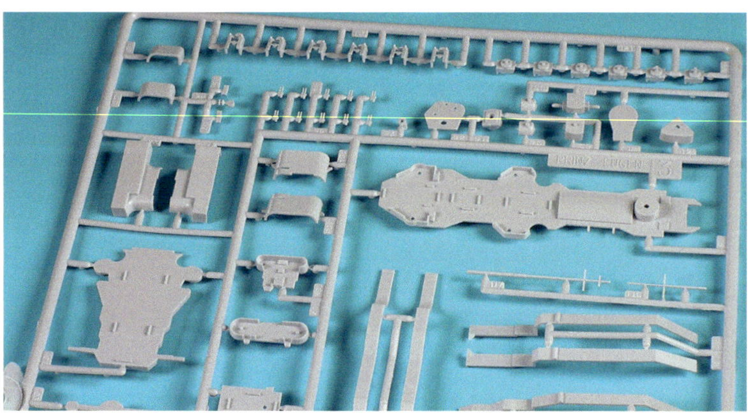

■ Sample: **Courtesy of Ted Bunn**

IRON SHIPWRIGHT *PRINZ EUGEN* 1:350 Scale

When released years ago, the Iron Shipwright *Prinz Eugen* in 1:350 scale was the largest commercially available model of any member of the *Hipper* class. Priced at over $300 US, the cruiser cost more than most battleship kits, but it certainly is a big model. The kit has been out of production for some time now and probably will never again be revived since Trumpeter has released their *Prinz Eugen* in

the same scale at about one-third of the price of the resin model. However, for those that have the ISW model they have something that was only produced in limited numbers. Many modellers prefer to work with resin as it is easy to sand and produces less seams than the equivalent plastic kit. The Iron Shipwright *Prinz Eugen*

has very good detail but even in this usual area of resin superiority the new Trumpeter kit has the edge. The model is of the cruiser's initial fit before the addition of *vierlings* and as such is optimised to portray the ship during *Operation Rheinübung*. However, it repeats the same error made by every other manufacturer of the *Prinz Eugen* except Hi Mold in having the forward HA directors covered with the spherical shield. In spite of being released about a decade ago, the Iron Shipwright *Prinz Eugen* has held up well but is no longer state of the art. Brass photo-etch comes with the ship so that eliminates the need to spend additional money on this necessary detail. However, even with factoring the additional expense of photo-etch detail for the Trumpeter *Prinz Eugen*, the plastic kit continues to hold a significant price advantage.

Sample: **Author's Collection**

TRUMPETER *PRINZ EUGEN* 1945 — 1:350 Scale

Although long in gestation, the Trumpeter 1:350 scale *Prinz Eugen* has finally arrived, shortly to be reinforced by an *Admiral Hipper*. In an odd choice Trumpeter has depicted the *Prinz Eugen* in her 1945 fit when her sole mission was using her heavy artillery to support the Wehrmacht. This fit certainly provides all the anti-aircraft guns that a Kriegsmarine fan would want, with all the 40mm single

Bofor guns in place – somewhat anaemic by 1945 USN cruiser standards but still the heaviest medium AA fit of any ship in the Kriegsmarine. Trumpeter can be hit or miss. Some of their 1:350 scale releases are excellent and yet some are on the south side of mediocre. Their *Prinz Eugen* is definitely top drawer. The kit provides two identical weapons sprues that contain the correct torpedo mounts for *Prinz Eugen* as well as the open mounts used in *Hipper*. Clearly, these sprues will also be included in the Trumpeter *Hipper* kit when released. Trumpeter has had a problem with fineness of detail in smaller AA guns but that is not true with the *Prinz Eugen*, which has the finest light AA yet produced by the company. The twin 105mm guns are especially notable in their execution. Hull, deck and superstructure detail is universally excellent, the only caveat being the large number of seams that will have to be filled. The kit has separate lower and upper hull parts so it can be built either waterline or full hull presentation. Some basic photo-etch is included, with railing, stack grate, inclined ladders, vertical ladders, as well as a few other details. However, there are no photo-etched radars and no matter how fine plastic parts are, they can never match the extremely fine detail of photo-etch. As a bonus a *S-100* Schnellboot is included in the kit. This kit is without doubt the best selection for those wanting a large, detailed model of the class.

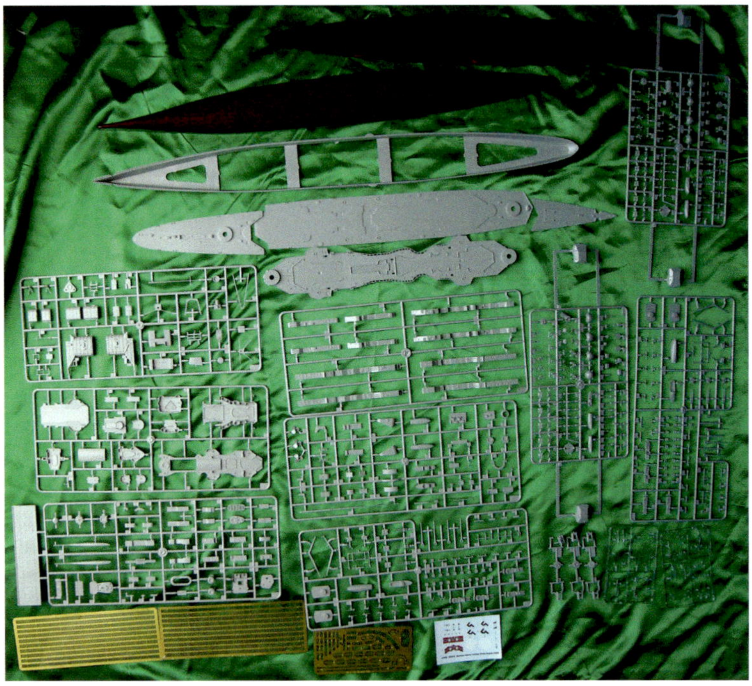

■ Sample: **Courtesy of Freetime Hobbies**
www.freetimehobbies.com

JSC *PRINZ EUGEN* 1:400 Scale

For decades card models have been extremely popular in Eastern Europe from Germany to Russia. There are a number of advantages to a card model. A large scale card model is very inexpensive compared to a plastic or resin model in the same scale and they are all printed in the camouflage or standard paint scheme so the model does not require painting. However, they do call for different skills from the modeller. To do it right, high control is needed to cut out the part accurately from the card sheet and then to bend it at exact locations. A higher degree of skill is required on smaller parts, as you have to form the part correctly before you get around to attaching it. Shown here is the first edition of the 1:400 scale *Prinz Eugen* published in 1996 from JSC of Poland. The cruiser is portrayed in her 1941 Baltic stripe scheme, which clearly shows the advantage of having the camouflage scheme printed onto the appropriate parts. JSC is in the process of releasing new, updated editions for *Hipper*, *Blücher* and *Prinz Eugen* and these new releases should be available by the time this volume is published.

■ Sample: **Author's Collection**

JSC *WESER*, EX *SEYDLITZ*

1:400 Scale

Now this is an off-beat topic but it fits into this volume on three counts. For one, the *Seydlitz* was to be the fourth sister of the class, and was 95 per cent complete when it was decided to remove all superstructure and turrets in order to convert the cruiser to an aircraft carrier. Secondly, plans were actually drafted and the order placed to complete the *Seydlitz* as the aircraft carrier *Weser*. Lastly, the quality of card models has increased dramatically since the JSC *Prinz Eugen* was published thirteen years ago, and this 1:400 scale model of the *Weser*, released in 2009, shows how much the art of card models has improved.

Sample: **Courtesy of JSC** www.jsc.pl

Photo-Etch & Accessories

FLYHAWK *PRINZ EUGEN* SHIP PHOTO-ETCH SET

1:700 Scale

This first release of a new photo-etch company is dedicated to detailing the Tamiya *Prinz Eugen*. Flyhawk Model of China has produced a three-fret set of brass photo-etch details for the kit, FH 700001. The A fret caters more to generic details than to *Prinz Eugen*-specific fittings. B Fret is loaded down with ship-specific details. If you like see-through bridge windows that can be glazed with Micro-Klear, this fret provides an alternate bridge with those open windows. C fret continues with the ship-specific parts. The detail on this fret are predominantly radar. All of the search and director arrays are provided. Some of these will be rather complex in assembly as there are individual dipoles provided. It is important to note that none of the frets come with deck railing, so you will still need that for complete coverage.

Sample: **Courtesy of Flyhawk Model**
http://www.flyhawkmodel.com

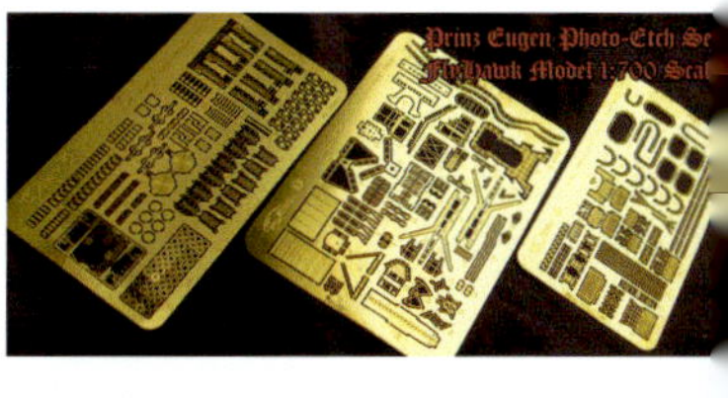

FLYHAWK KRIEGSMARINE PORTHOLES AND WINDOWS

1:700 Scale

In addition to producing brass photo-etch sets for specific kits, Flyhawk Model also produces general fittings and ordnance frets. Flyhawk Model set FH 700003 set consists of seven styles of scuttles found in the warships of the Kriegsmarine. All of these portholes are relief etched, and include the rigol (eyebrow). One style is without a porthole cover, but all of the others include one. Four styles are standard round portholes but with the cover hinged at different points. The last two styles are square windows with covers hinged at the side or on the bottom.

Sample: **Courtesy of Flyhawk Model**
http://www.flyhawkmodel.com

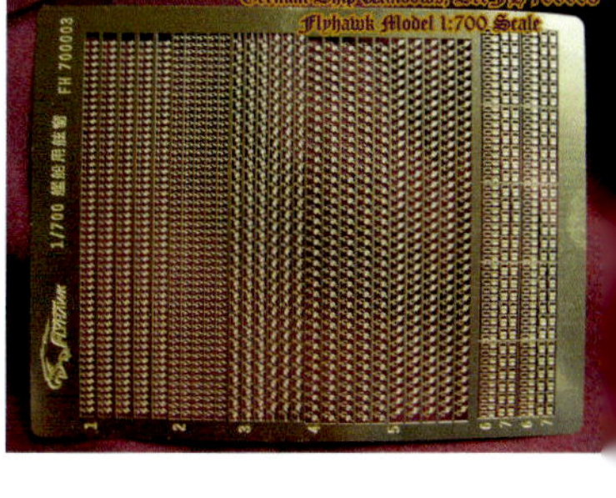

FLYHAWK 40mm BOFORS GUNS 1:700 Scale

The Germans acquired 40mm Bofors guns late in the war. Flyhawk Model has produced a 1:700 scale brass photo-etch set of this ordnance. Flyhawk set FH 700013 provides 22 of these mounts. Each gun comprises four different relief-etched parts: gun, shield, base and forward cradle. The gun part folds to also provide gun sights while the shield part also folds to provide gunner's seats. Instructions show the 40mm/28 gun positions on the 1945 fit of the heavy cruiser *Prinz Eugen*.

Sample: **Courtesy of Flyhawk Model** http://www.flyhawkmodel.com

LION ROAR BRASS NAME PLATES 1:700 Scale

With six nameplates per set, Lion Roar had to choose which warships would be most popular. For the Kriegsmarine set LE 700072, the selections were obvious – the four battleships *Bismarck*, *Tirpitz*, *Scharnhorst*, *Gneisenau*, plus the most famous panzerschiffe *Graf Spee* and the heavy cruiser *Prinz Eugen*.

Sample: **Courtesy of Lion Roar** www.lionroar.net

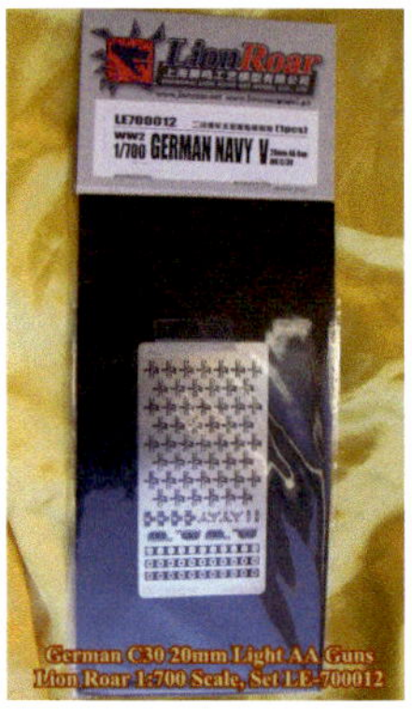

LION ROAR DETAIL SET FOR THE SINGLE 20mm C30 AA GUNS 1:700 Scale

Lion Roar has produced a stainless steel photo-etch set in 1:700 scale, which provides 52 of the C30 20mm German light AA guns, set LE 700012. Since the C38 version looked the same as the earlier C30, these photo-etch parts could be used for the C38 guns as well. Lion Roar has designed the guns so that extra width is provided to the breech-block and pedestal by providing an extra layer for the thicker parts of the gun. The base plates are also part of each one-piece gun and fold outwards from the base of the pedestal. On this fret Lion Roar also throws in a small assortment of miscellaneous DKM fittings.

Sample: **Courtesy of Lion Roar** www.lionroar.net

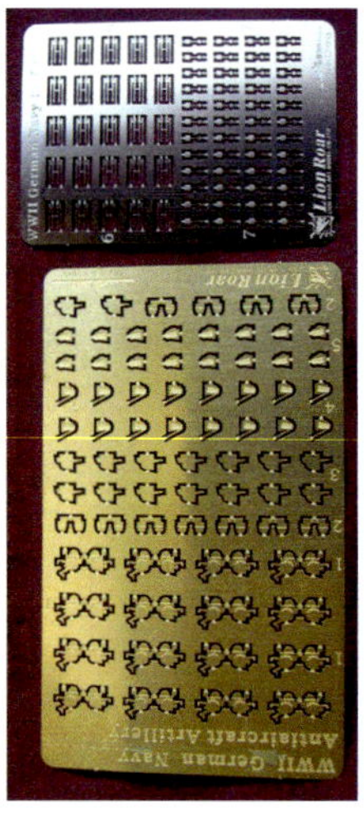

LION ROAR DETAIL SET FOR THE QUADRUPLE 20mm VIERLING 1:700 Scale

The Kriegsmarine developed their own weapons for light AA defence, when other navies went for the Swiss-designed Oerlikon. In 1940 a new mount was developed to further increase armament. Designed by Mauser and produced by Rheinmetall, the weapon was the very effective quad 20mm. Known as the *2cm Flak 35 im Vierling L/38*, the new mount had four C38 guns on a new mount. The German *Vierling* was an excellent light AA system and was mounted on the *Prinz Eugen*, or *Hipper*. Lion Roar has produced a two-fret set of photo-etched *Vierling* in 1:700 scale, set LE 700013. This set consists of two frets of relief-etched parts. The larger of the two frets is of brass and contains five different types of parts to assemble the chassis of the mount. The smaller fret is of stainless steel and contains the gun barrels and gunners' seats. A total of sixteen quad 20mm mounts can be assembled from this set but only eleven can have gun shields on the front, as the brass fret provides only that number of shields.

Sample: **Courtesy of Lion Roar** www.lionroar.net

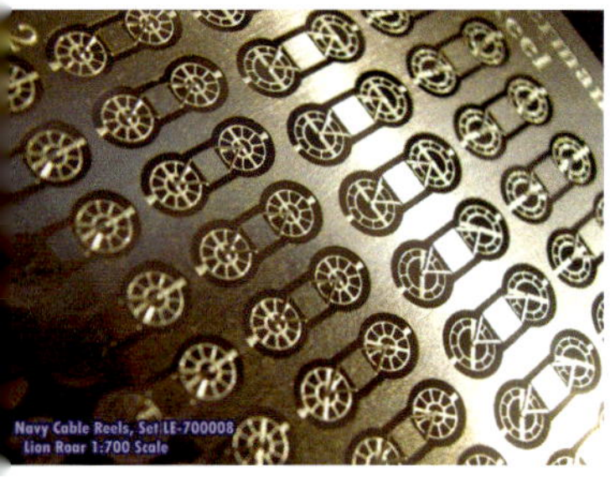

LION ROAR DETAIL SET FOR THE CABLE/HOSE REELS 1:700 Scale

Warships of the Deutsche Kriegsmarine, in common with the ships of other nations, had a significant number of cable and hose reels as fittings on the deck or on the side of bulkheads. Although cable reels are found in some resin and brass 1:700 kits, they are very rarely found as acceptable detail in plastic kits; if they are present at all, they are more likely to resemble amorphous blobs. Lion Roar has released a brass photo-etch set that will supply you with detailed cable and hose reels for your 1:700 scale German warship kits, including *Bismarck* and *Tirpitz*, whether they are in plastic or resin. Lion Roar photo-etch set LE 700008 is devoted just to cable reels of the Kriegsmarine. The brass fret contains reels in three different sizes. There are sixteen large reels, eighteen medium size reels and thirty-six small reels. Although the medium and small reels appear to share the same basic design, the large reels are completely different in design. All seventy reels in the fret are relief-etched with the reel frame overlapping the reel ends.

■ Sample: **Courtesy of Lion Roar** www.lionroar.net

MASTER MODEL TURNED BRASS BARRELS FOR 4.1in (105mm) GUNS

1:350 Scale

Master Model set SM 003 provides finely turned brass barrels in 1:350 scale for the secondary or heavy anti-aircraft gun barrels. Sixteen in number, despite of their small size they to have open muzzles, providing the best quality appearance. These barrels are for the early C/31 open mount found on all of the 4.1in/105mm mounts of all three cruisers completed.

■ Sample: **Courtesy of AAA Model Hobbies** http://stores.shop.ebay.com/AAA-Model-Hobbies

WHITE ENSIGN MODELS *ADMIRAL HIPPER* CLASS

1:700 Scale

This photo-etch set, PE 744, is the perfect complement for any of the 1:700 scale kits available, providing necessary relief-etched parts for all three cruisers. Two different types of crane are provided, as *Prinz Eugen* had a different design from the other two, and there is also the specific funnel platform with its multiple supports for *Hipper/Blücher*. Catapult and catapult rail, plus Arado detail will spruce up the hangar area. All of the necessary radar aerials for the ships can be found, as well as eagle stern crests. Another very noticeable design feature found in this set are the midship battery elevation stop rails. With all of the different types of railing, ladders, Marx floats and more, all of the generic items are covered. This set is perfect to further detail any model from the *Hipper* class.

■ Sample: **Courtesy of White Ensign Models** www.whiteensignmodels.com

WHITE ENSIGN MODELS *ADMIRAL HIPPER* CLASS

1:400 Scale

White Ensign Models PE 4003 is not just an enlarged version of their 1:700 fret, as it provides more parts as well as all of the same items found on the smaller fret. Beautiful relief-etched AA crown turret platforms provide the base for *vierling* mounts; in fact, you do not have to make do with any of the plastic AA gun parts supplied by Heller as the set provides *vierlings*, 37mm mounts, 20mm single mounts and 40mm Bofors guns (for the late war fit of *Prinz Eugen*). The tower bridge gets a makeover with navigation wings for the bridge with supports and footrails. All of the features for a late-war main mast are also provided. This is an absolutely essential set for completing either of the Heller kits.

■ Sample: **Courtesy of White Ensign Models** www.whiteensignmodels.com

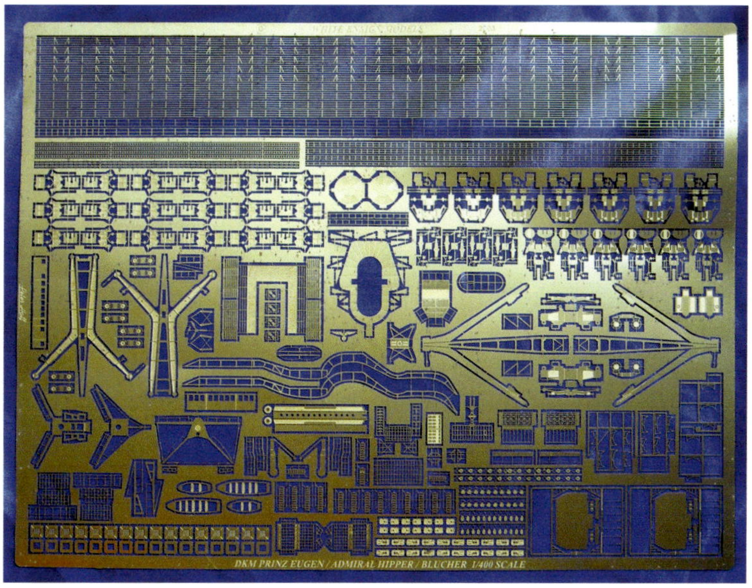

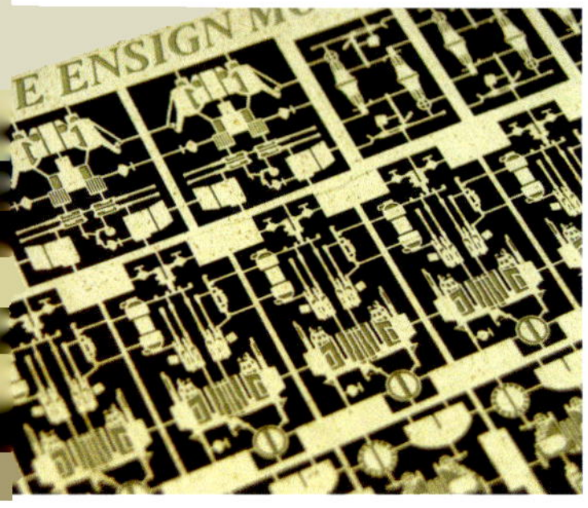

WHITE ENSIGN MODELS DKM ANTI-AIRCRAFT WEAPONS

1:700 and 1:350 Scale

More essentials are provided with PE 733: single gun 20mm mounts and the four-barrelled *vierling* mounts. No Bofors are included and the 37mm mounts found on the fret are late-war versions, not carried by the *Hipper* class. PE 3566 provides the same mounts found in the 1:700 scale version, except the appropriate C30 37mm mount for the *Hipper* class is included. Extensive relief-etching is used throughout both sets.

Sample: **Courtesy of White Ensign Models**
www.whiteensignmodels.com

WHITE ENSIGN MODELS DKM ANTI-AIRCRAFT WEAPONS

1:400 Scale

If you do not get the specific WEM 1:400 scale ship set, WEM PE 4006 provides five types of light AA weapons on this fret. There are fourteen single 20mm guns, 2cm Flak C30, each of which consists of three parts: pedestal with hand-wheel, barrel with folding shoulder rests and ammunition clip. There are ten twin 20mm mounts, each of which has seven parts – barrels with folding shoulder rests, pedestal, two ammunition clips, half shield, full shield and base plate. There are six of the quad 20mm mounts, 2cm *Flakvierling*, each with seven parts – two twin barrels, mount, two shield halves, base with two folding gunner's seats and a separate

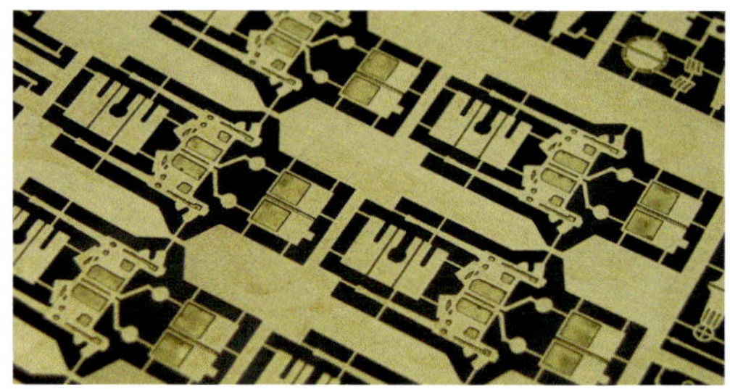

site/gunner's seat piece. You have to shape the centre part of the mount from resin scrap or plasticard.

Sample: **Courtesy of White Ensign Models**
www.whiteensignmodels.com

WHITE ENSIGN MODELS DKM PORTHOLES AND DOORS

1:400 and 1:350 Scale

The 1:400 scale photo-etch brass fret of Kriegsmarine portholes, doors and hatches (PE 4012) provides a tremendous variety of these overlooked fittings. Each and every one is magnificently relief-etched. The fret contains: 28 doors with open portholes; 2 small doors/hatches; 76 rectangular windows in three different styles; and 127 round portholes in three different styles with eyebrows. All of the windows and portholes have the solid cover open from the frame so the modeller can depict the aperture open or closed. It will take patience to attach these portholes, one at a time, over the featureless holes on the Heller *Prinz Eugen* or *Hipper* kits but they will pump up the detail of either kit dramatically. PE 3579 gives you the same treatment but in 1:350 scale. Both the Iron Shipwright and Trumpeter kits will benefit from this detail.

Sample: **Courtesy of White Ensign Models**
www.whiteensignmodels.com

WHITE ENSIGN MODELS DKM PORTHOLES AND DOORS

1:700 Scale

This set is not a smaller version of the White Ensign Models DKM Portholes and Doors set in 1:400 scale. All doors and windows are in the closed position with WEM PE 764 and concentrates on doors. There are 140 doors in five different patterns and 34 square windows. All of these small brass parts are beautifully executed with fine relief-etching.

Sample: **Courtesy of White Ensign Models**
www.whiteensignmodels.com

WHITE ENSIGN MODELS CABLE REELS

1:700, 1/400 and 1/350 Scale

Every navy had its own designs for cable reels and these fittings were very common on any warship. White Ensign Models provides individual cable reel sets in 1:700 (PE 786), 1:400 (PE 4013) and 1:350 (PE 35107). Each set provides nine different Kriegsmarine reel designs. Quantities vary by scale with the most parts provided in the 1:700 scale set.

Sample: **Courtesy of White Ensign Models**
www.whiteensignmodels.com

Modelmakers' Showcase

TAMIYA *PRINZ EUGEN* 1:700 scale

By JOSEPH REINDLER

Joseph Reindler writes: Here are some photographs of my completed model of the 1:700 scale Tamiya *Prinz Eugen*. I chose to model *Der Prinz*, the famous German heavy cruiser and bane of the Royal Navy, as during the Denmark Straits battle of 24 May 1941 where she played an important role in the destruction of HMS *Hood*. As such, the camouflage and general fit of the model are specific to this date. I needed no motivation in choosing to build this particular ship; I did, however, need plenty of motivation to actually finish it. I bought the Tamiya kit shortly after seeing Melvin Tung's astounding and awe-inspiring build of the model in late-war fit on PrinzEugen.com and Melvin's work was actually my inspiration for this earlier version. In my opinion the DKM *Prinz Eugen* was perhaps the most handsome warship ever built, and the ships of the *Admiral Hipper* class were very advanced, powerful and heavily armed designs for their day. But the single factor that made *Prinz Eugen* the most attractive of the three sisters to build was her illustrious WWII career.

I used the Tamiya model as the base for my build, as it is in my opinion the best model available anywhere of this ship. The Tamiya kit is nothing short of superb even out of the box – frankly, it demonstrates how other 1:700 plastic kit manufacturers really have a lot of catching up to do. I fitted my *Prinz* mainly with photo-etch parts from

White Ensign Models and some scratch built bits and pieces to fill in the shortfalls of the WEM fret. The WEM *Admiral Hipper* class and WWII KM AA frets were the guts of what I had to use to make this model into what it is now. I should add that I also added crew figures and cable reels that came from Gold Medal Models.

The major changes I made to the ship through scratch-building were to the fire-control stations flanking the bridge – where the four hooded-cover versions were incorrect for the May 1941 sortie, and needed to be changed to the open configurations. These cylindrical shields I actually made from tubular plastic *lollypop sticks*, and the director booms from photo-etch fret off-cuts and borders. I also hacked off the very heavy boat deck motor-launch racks, and replaced these with thin strips of brass that I cut off my WEM fret borders. I constructed my own paravanes after coming to the conclusion that all of the plastic spares I had looked terrible. Does anybody actually make these for sale in good quality I wonder? To do this I took brass pin nails, and used the points of the nail to model the taper. I cut off the heads and rounded the stump into a nice round bulb with my file and emory-paper. The brass was soft enough to work with and the fins were easy enough to cut out from photo-etch fret borders again.

Other than these changes, the remainder of the numerous alterations to the model I made were a lot subtler and perhaps harder to notice. I scratch-built the optical apparatus placed around the bridge decks from stretched sprue and *plastruct-plasticard*. I used WEM 1-bar handrails to create the horizontal railing around the funnel and bridge decks. I drilled extra portholes and made covers from a thick piece of stretched sprue. I added extra scuttles and deck fittings from brass border scrap and plastic off-cuts etc. The searchlights I eventually patterned with the three horizontal spars by painting them black, then affixed stretched sprue using Gunze-Sanjo matt acrylic varnish. Rigging is stretched-sprue ... but to be honest, given the length of time it took me to build this model, I can't actually remember everything else that I have done to it.

As for guns, guns always mean a lot to me – especially when they needed to be accurate for the Denmark Strait battle – so I took special interest in them. I used the plastic kit 20.3cm barrels, but bored out the ends carefully with my trusty X-acto instrument. The blast bags I made from Tamiya epoxy putty, and (open) sighting ports on the turret faces from 1:700 photo-etch ladders. All of the light AA are from the KM AA WEM fret. The single 40mm mounts included in the Tamiya kit were left out, since this extra armament was only added to the ship late in the war. The 105mm HA artillery looked good enough just out of the box – the only change I made was to add the hatches on the sides of each turret. I did not change the torpedoes and launchers at all – I only added some crew to each mount. I know that during the final stages of the Denmark Strait battle *Prinz Eugen* attempted to close for a torpedo attack on the *Prince of Wales*. Hence

I thought that manning these launchers was reasonable enough.

Further armament detail specific to the Denmark Straits battle included the quarterdeck depth charge rack. Several photos taken aboard *Prinz Eugen*, looking aft across the deck clearly show that the rack was used, and that charges were either dropped into the water – or taken off the rack, disarmed and stowed. From my research I could come to no conclusions as to what the *Prinz Eugen* was doing with her depth charges. It did occur to me however, that perhaps the *Prinz Eugen* was dropping charges in the water just to confuse the British gunners, as a charge set to explode at a shallow depth would look just like a shell splash – and would have fooled the British gunners into thinking that their ordinance was landing much closer than it really was. Of course I may have this wrong but this was my theory behind the depth charge rack. I was only having some fun with it after all.

I tried to be realistic with the placing of my crew figures. From what I have read about the Kriegsmarine, during any surface engagement there would be very few crew standing about aimlessly on the decks. I do know, however, that the ship would have had 'intensified lookouts' and crew manning every other gun position. You will notice in one photo a signalman in the bridge-wing with two orange flags; again I was really just having a little fun with this one, as there is a well known photo taken from *Prinz*, where the signalman is communicating with the *Bismarck* – I know that there were escorting destroyers that were off to the starboard side of this ship, so I am assuming that they are being signalled to, to warn of a course change – or perhaps an imminent torpedo run. I painted the model with airbrushed coats of WEM colours: Hellgrau 50, Teak etc, and then weathered these with thin hand-brushed washes of Tamiya and Citadel acrylics.

As for the photography, I hope these shots will suffice. I do not put my models into sea-bases because the big kid in me still likes to sail them across the living room floor and into battle. I photographed my model with my Canon A300 digi-cam, together with my ever-expanding collection of interesting Kriegsmarine junk. I have varied lighting in the photos, but it is mostly natural – only two of the close-ups were taken under artificial light and flash.

As an honest confession, this model has taken me two and a half years to build – but this is really because I am a full time student, and I do have other, mostly less moral, hobbies as well. This was also the first model I ever put photo-etched parts on; but I have been building model warships since I was about four. I am currently under serious pressure from my friends to build *Bismarck* to go with *Prinz* – so I guess this one I'll work on in the near future, time and money permitting.

H-P MODELS ***ADMIRAL HIPPER*** AND ***BLÜCHER*** 1:700 scale

By CHRISTOPH MENTZEL

Christoph Mentzel writes: The *Admiral Hipper* class kits from H-P Models are some of the earlier kits from that company. Nevertheless they are not bad kits. By today's standards there are a lot of improvements possible, but at the time the kits were done by H-P some information was not available. H-P Models have produced all three ships of this class and overall they have done a good job on them. Every kit is specific and shows the main differences between the three sisters.

All three kits have a different hull and this is one of the best features of the kit. They are nicely cast and include details on the hull sides. The resin upperworks are also acceptable, but as with most H-P Models they are cast level by level for the decks without any help-lines on the decks for the correct positioning of the parts. So the modeller needs good research information and photographs to get it right. It is more difficult to build a H-P kit than newer kits in which most of the upperworks are cast on the hull.

The weapons, I must say, are nearly all bad and the main weakness of the kits. The 20.3cm turrets are totally wrong and have to be replaced. All other weapons are a little over-scale, but today most of them can be replaced with several aftermarket sets. The H-P Model kits of the *Admiral Hipper* and the *Blücher* are a good starting point to build these ships which are different in many aspects. By using brass photo-etch sets it is possible to make a good model from any of them.

TAMIYA ***PRINZ EUGEN*** 1:700 scale

By MELVIN TUNG

Melvin Tung from Taiwan built this Tamiya 1:700 scale model *Prinz Eugen* using PrinzEugen.com as a reference. White Ensign Models *Admiral Hipper* class photo-etch set was used throughout the model. The model was modified to show the ship as she appeared in 1945 with 40mm Bofors guns. To provide for the 1945 fit, Melvin scratch-built all eighteen of these 40mm single gun mounts. Melvin now runs Veteran Models and produces some of the best ordnance and equipment fittings in the world, as well as having complete resin ship kits in 1:700 scale. Notice the incredible detail that can be added even to a 1:700 scale kit, such as individual porthole covers, funnel handrail and strap-downs for Marx floats.

TAMIYA *PRINZ EUGEN* 1:700 scale By CHARLES MATTHEWS

Photo-etch was added from White Ensign Models. In addition, various other details were added such as brass deck supports, brass mast bracing, and photo-etch crane rigging, etc. The model represents the cruiser as she appeared at the start of the encounter with *Hood*. Notice that the forward HA director positions, on either side of the tower, correctly lack the spherical protective covers but that the torpedo mounts incorrectly have open crew positions instead of the proper enclosed cabs.

IRON SHIPWRIGHT *PRINZ EUGEN* 1:350 scale

By BOB LaPADURA

As a full hull ship the cruiser is impressively large in this scale. The model clearly shows the beautiful lines of the class and especially of the *Prinz Eugen* with her extremely raked and graceful clipper bow. Portrayed for *Operation Rheinübung*, there should have been no protective covers over the forward HA towers. The kit most accurately depicts the cruiser from June 1941 when she received her spherical covers on the forward HA positions in Brest, France until December 1941 when she received the first of her four-barrelled *vierling* mounts. There should be a searchlight mounted on the upper tower platform. A searchlight was mounted at this position until January 1942 when replaced by a *vierling*.

Arado Ar 196

All colour artwork © Eric Leon 2010

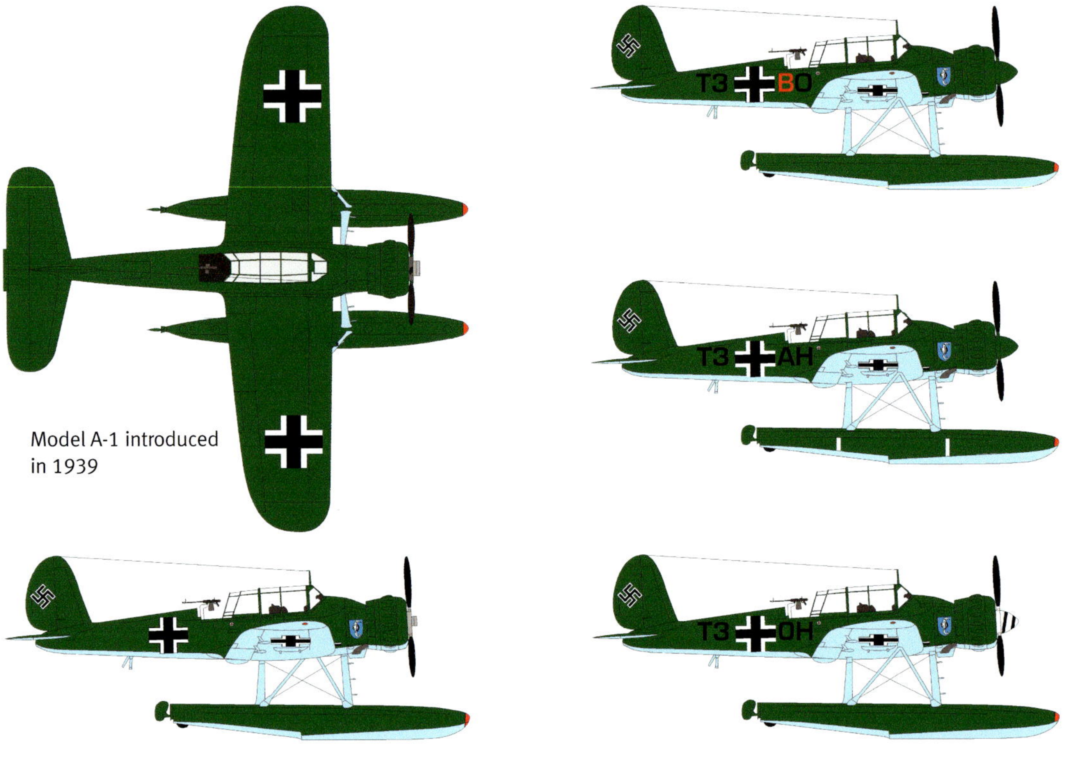

Model A-1 introduced in 1939

The markings of three Model A-3 aircraft carried by *Prinz Eugen* at different times, but exact dates unknown

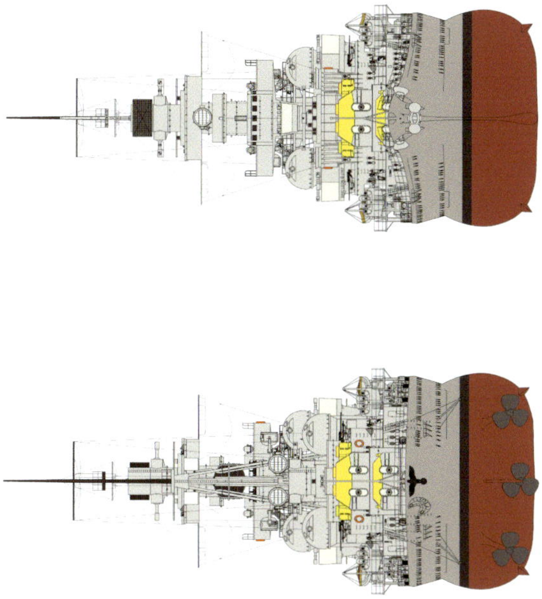

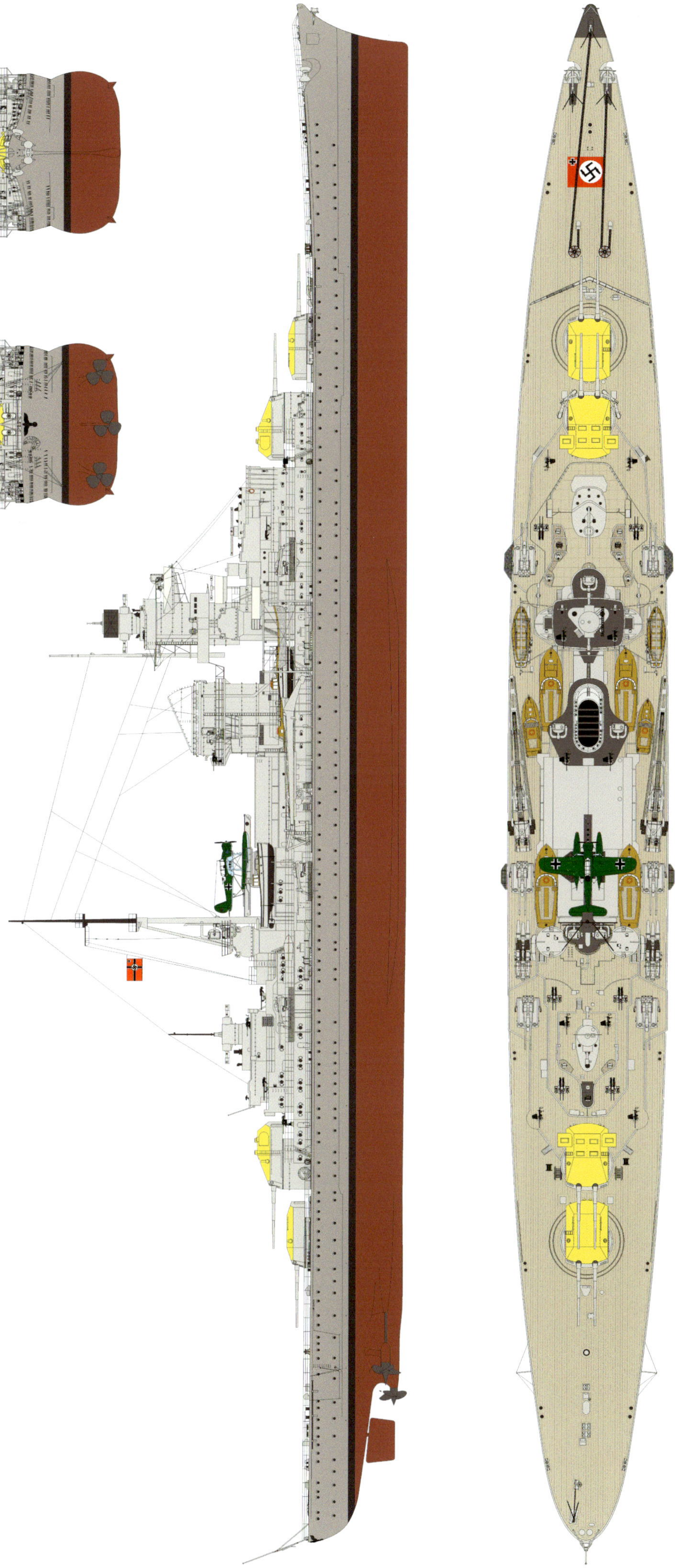

Blücher April 1940
Colour scheme for the invasion of Norway, *Operation Weserübung*

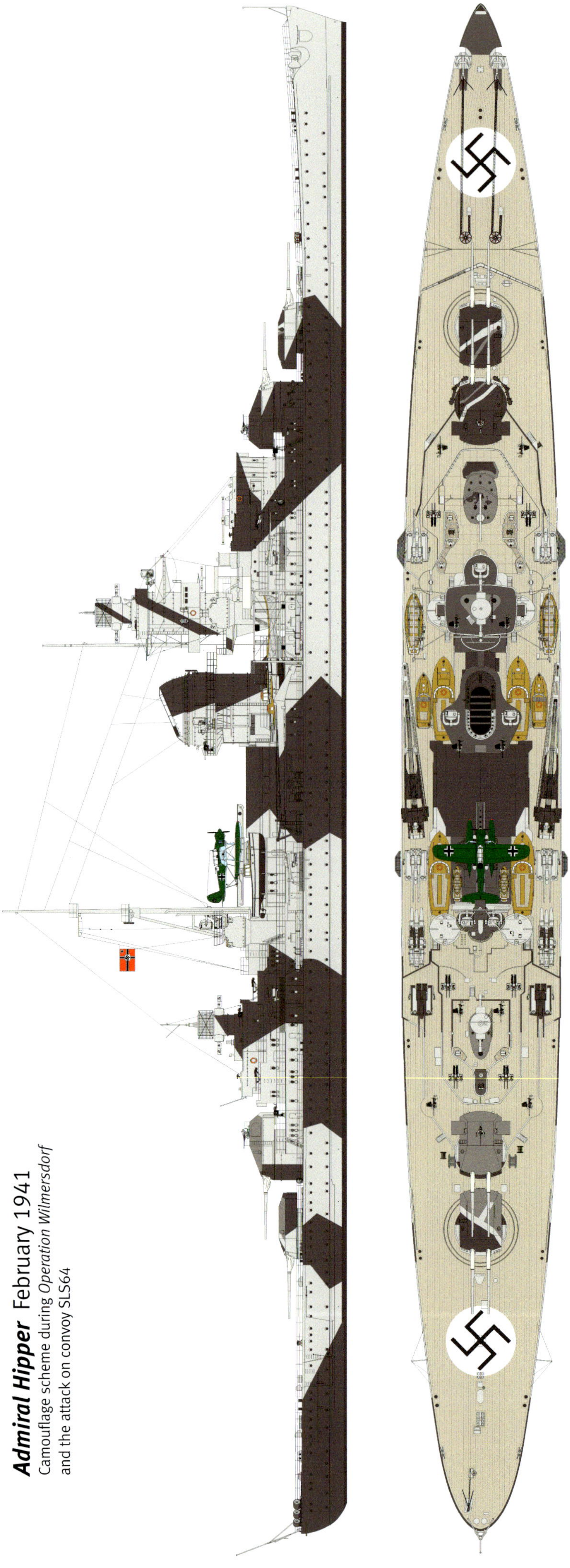

Admiral Hipper February 1941
Camouflage scheme during *Operation Wilmersdorf* and the attack on convoy SLS64

Admiral Hipper July 1942
Camouflage scheme during *Operation Rösselsprung*, the attack on convoy PQ17

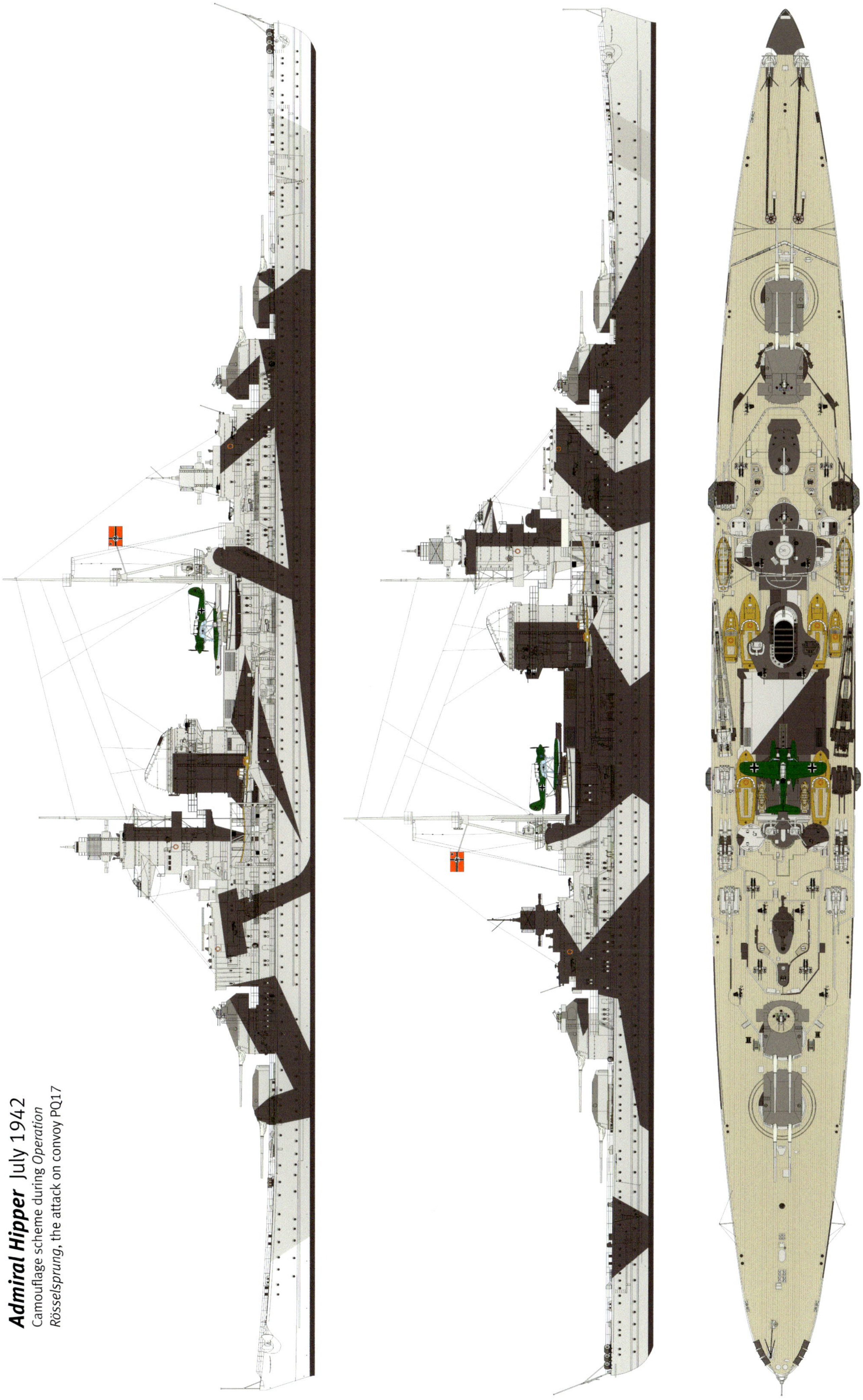

Admiral Hipper July 1942
Camouflage scheme during *Operation Rösselsprung*, the attack on convoy PQ17

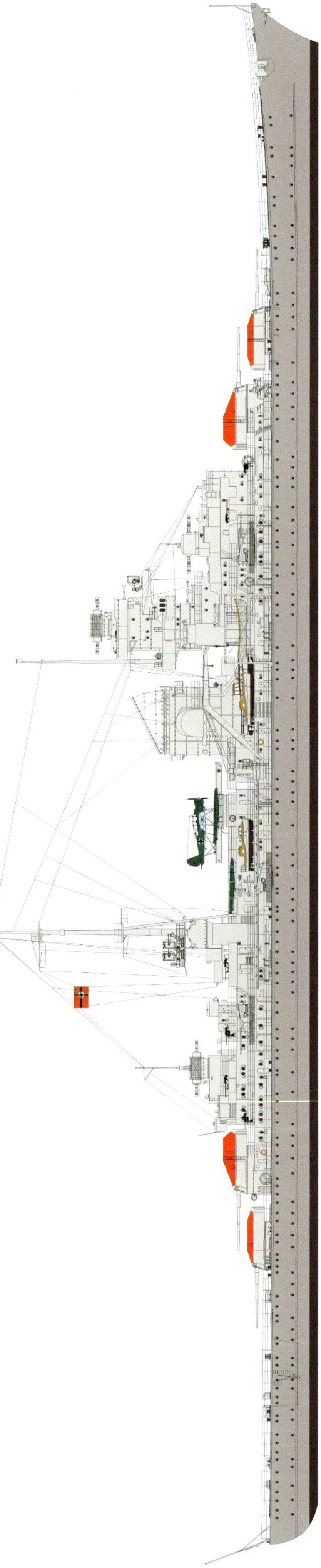

Prinz Eugen October 1940
Colour scheme carried during trials and working up

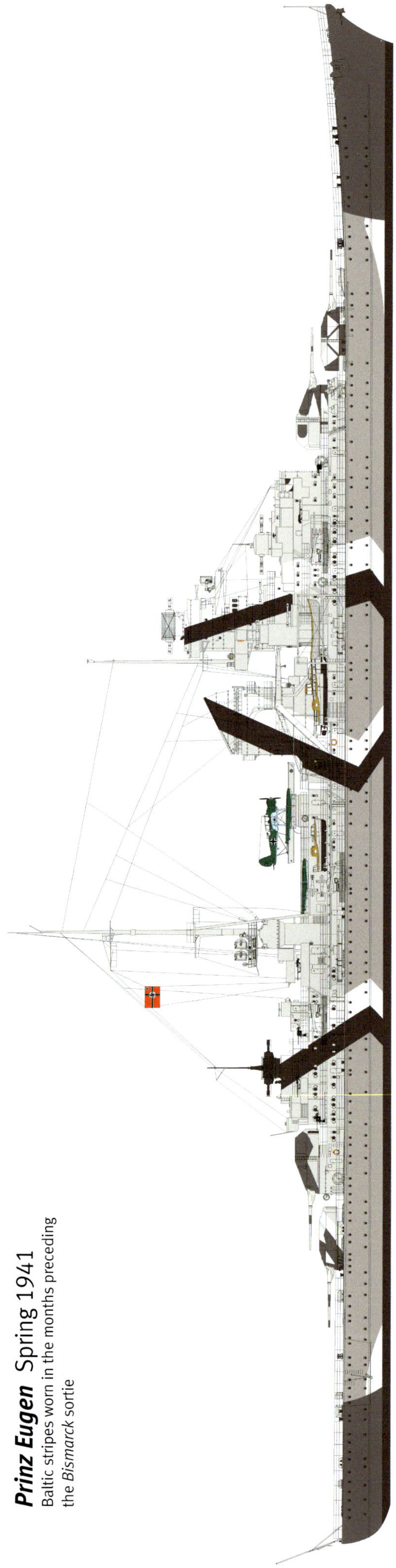

Prinz Eugen Spring 1941
Baltic stripes worn in the months preceding the *Bismarck* sortie

Prinz Eugen May 1941

As repainted immediately before *Operation Rheinübung*, the *Bismarck* sortie. Note the ghostly image of the earlier dark colours still visible beneath the grey over-painting.

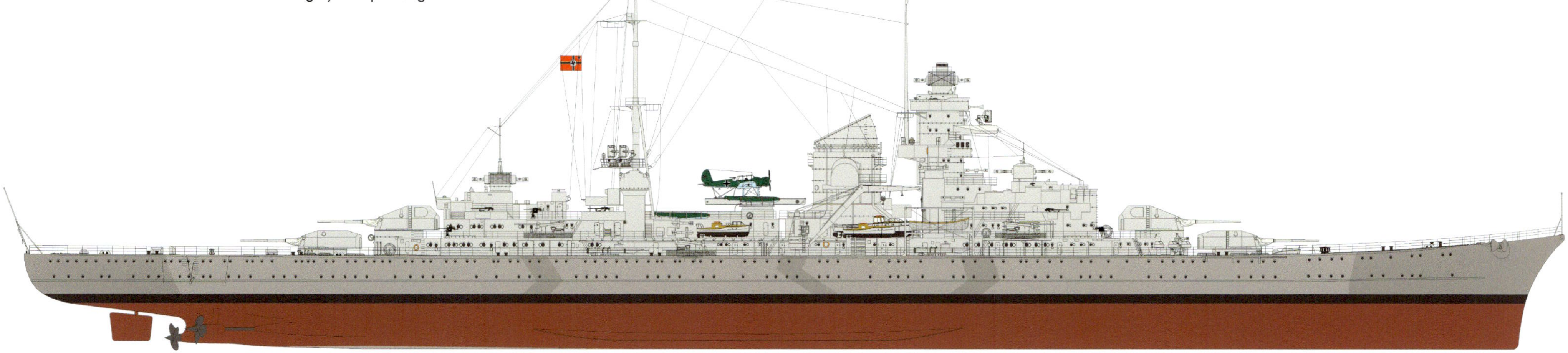

Prinz Eugen mid February 1942

Probable appearance during the Channel Dash

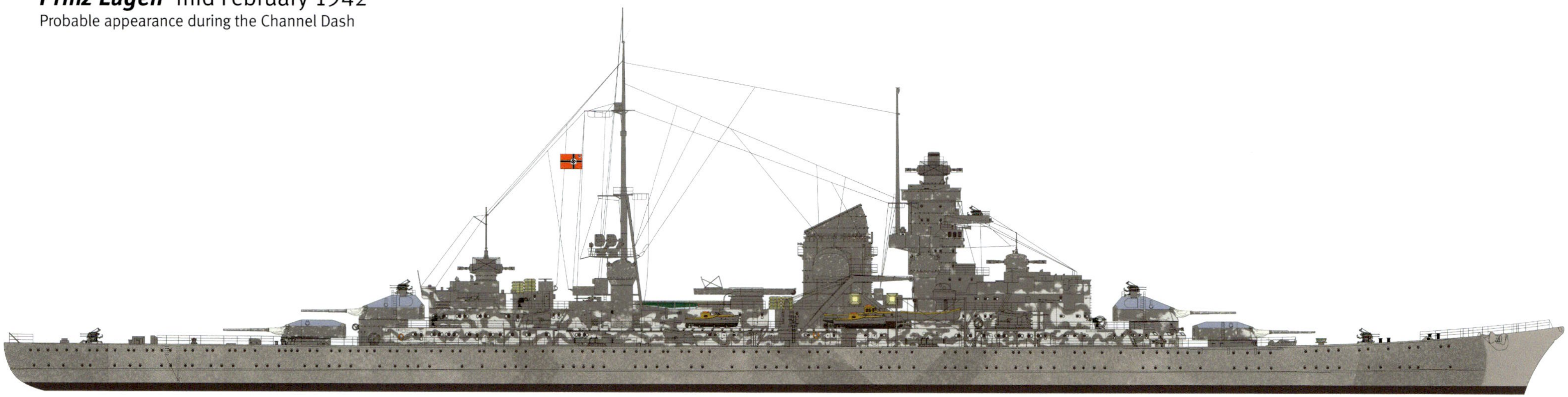

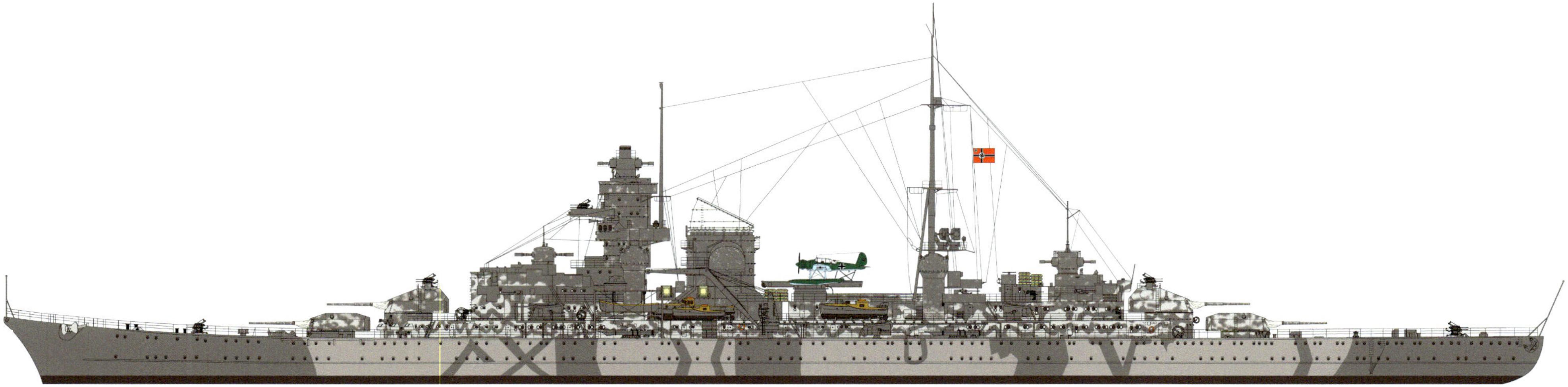

Prinz Eugen late February 1942
Camouflage (port and starboard patterns) for Norway deployment, when torpedoed by HMS/M *Trident*

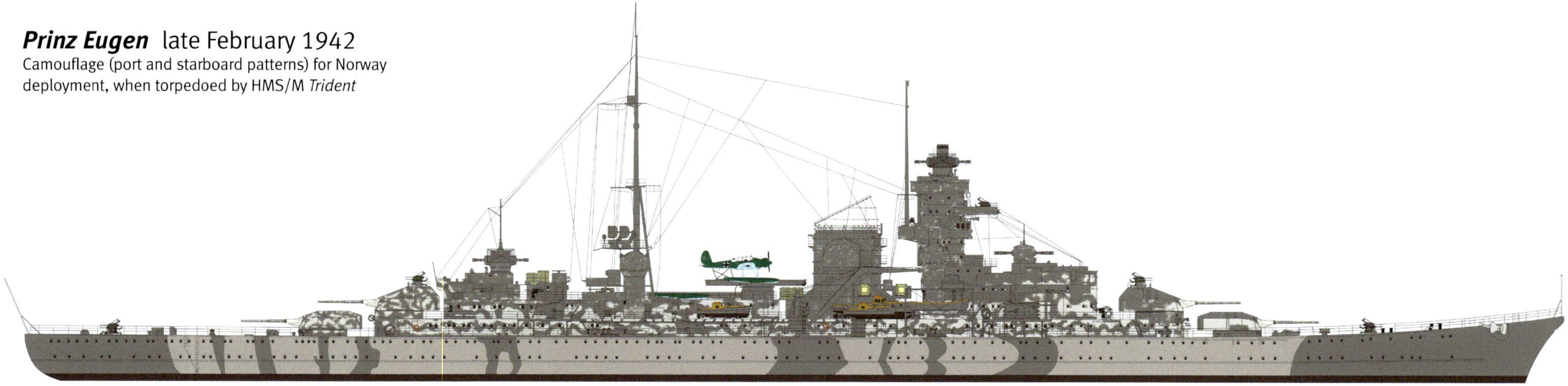

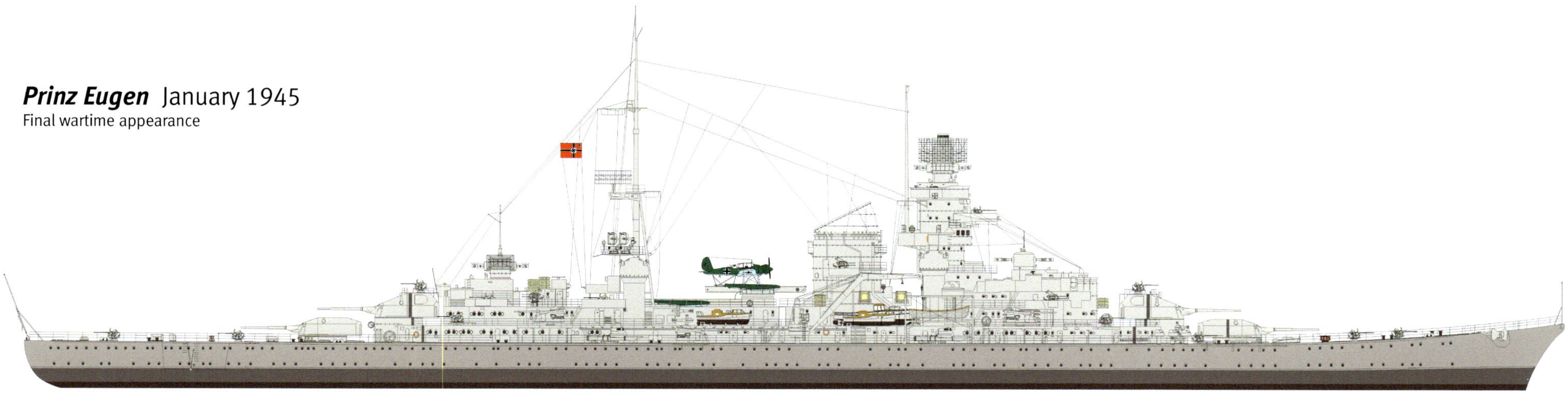

Prinz Eugen January 1945
Final wartime appearance

Above: *Prinz Eugen* was named after the Duke of Marlborough's great ally during the War of Spanish Succession, known in English-language history as Prince Eugene of Savoy. As the leader of the Imperial forces in that conflict, he was claimed as their hero by the Austro-Hungarian empire, who named a battleship after him during the First World War. Adopting the name for the German cruiser was a political sop to Austria, which had been absorbed into the Third Reich a few months before the ship's launch in 1938. The ship carried the bell of the old KuK battleship *Tegetthoff*, and the main turrets were named after Austrian cities – from forward, Graz, Braunau, Innsbruck and Wien – whose names were carried in gothic script on the turret faces, as shown in this October 1940 view.

Eugene is probably unique among historical personages in having warships named after him in four major navies, including the British monitor *Prince Eugene* and the Italian cruiser *Eugenio di Savoia*.

A recent photo of the upturned wreck of the *Prinz Eugen* at Kwajalein Island in the south Pacific.

Left: *Prinz Eugen* at sea in October 1940. Note the colour of the turret tops and the swastika on the forecastle.

Below: The *Admiral Hipper* was badly damaged at Kiel by a massive RAF bomber raid on 9 April 1945 and repairs were never completed before the war's end. This colour photo of the bombed-out wreck was taken at Kiel in June 1945.

Appearance

ATLANTIK BOW AND FUNNEL CAP

In World War Two German ships had common characteristics that made it difficult to distinguish one ship class from another. This 'family resemblance' was intentional, as naval command knew that this would enhance operational security and make it difficult for an enemy to keep track of the individual ships. These characteristics consisted of a sharply raked clipper bow, which the Germans called the *Atlantik* bow, prominent forward superstructure tower, and single funnel with raked funnel cap. However, this was not the original family appearance. With the construction of *Deutschland*, *Admiral Scheer* and *Admiral Graf Spee*, the ships did have the single stack and tower superstructure but had a straight stem and a flat top on the stack instead of having a raked cap. The *Scharnhorst* and *Bismarck* class battleships were also started with straight stems, as were four of the five cruisers of the *Hipper* class. As the *Scharnhorst*, *Gneisenau* and *Hipper* started trials, it quickly became apparent that they were very wet forward. At high speed the forecastle would take a lot of water over the bow because the straight stem did not divert the waves from the deck. This may not have been noticed with the *panzerschiffe*, as those diesel-powered ships were significantly slower than the steam turbine designs for *Scharnhorst* and *Hipper*.

As a consequence, a new bow was designed for every type of heavy ship under construction. The new raked and flared *Atlantik* bow was designed to have the hollow under the deck edge direct the water back to the sea, rather than having it cascade over the forecastle. Although far more graceful than a straight stem, the new bow was only partially successful in its designed purpose. *Scharnhorst*, *Gneisenau* and *Hipper* were retro-fitted with the new bow. *Blücher*, *Prinz Eugen* and *Seydlitz*, having already been launched, were given

Admiral Hipper's bow was less extreme than the design fitted to her sisters. The cutwater was neither as raked, nor was there as much flare, its shape demonstrated clearly in this view of the ship in drydock in late April 1940 at Wilhelmshaven, for repairs to the damage caused by HMS *Glowworm*. Note the painted-over ship's crest.

Prinz Eugen was fitted with a heavily raked version of the *Atlantik* bow, shown off here by the ship in Lo Fjord, Norway, during May 1942 trials with the temporary rudders fitted after the stern was blown off by a submarine torpedo.

Above: *Blücher*'s bow was similar to that of *Prinz Eugen* but slightly broader and more rounded at the stemhead. Note the prominent stem anchor in this view of the ship taken early in 1940, while still working up

Above, right: A close-up of the modified funnel with its cap, seen on *Prinz Eugen* in 1944.

their clipper bows during fitting out. Only *Lützow* was still on the ways and received the clipper bow before launch. The cruisers were fitted with a ship's crest in the form of the namesake's coat of arms. With the straight prow the crest faced forward at the stemhead, but with the introduction of the *Atlantik* bow, the single crest was replaced with two shields, one on each side. When war erupted, these were painted grey for operational security purposes.

Another problem with the original designs for *Scharnhorst* and *Hipper* was the flat top of the stack. During trials, both the battleship and the cruiser experienced the same problem in that exhaust fumes would often be drawn into the forward tower and interfere with crew operations. The most

Funnel, hangar and back of the bridge details for *Admiral Hipper* in March 1941. The ship is in drydock at Brest, receiving minor repairs and supplies.

likely reason that this defect in design did not appear in the *panzerschiffe* was again the motive power. Diesel engines produced less exhaust, which had a lower heat, than the exhaust that came straight from firing the boilers in a steam turbine design, and higher speeds created a greater draft. A sharply raked and handsome funnel cap was added to the *Scharnhorst*, *Gneisenau* and *Hipper*, which were already in service, and the remaining cruisers had one added during fitting out. The additions of the clipper bow and funnel cap created a new 'family resemblance'. *Scheer* and *Lützow* (as the *Deutschland* was renamed after the cruiser *Lützow* was transferred to Russia) were subsequently given these same features. However, the *Atlantik* bows fitted to *Hipper*, *Blücher* and *Prinz Eugen* differed in detail. The bow on *Hipper* had far less of a rake than that found on the other two. Likewise, there was a very slightly greater rake with the bow of *Prinz Eugen* over that of *Blücher*. The deck at the top of the cutwater of *Blücher* was slightly wider and rounded when compared to that of *Prinz Eugen*, which ended in a much sharper tip. Additionally, the deck hawse for the forward anchor of *Blücher* was larger than that on *Prinz Eugen*.

SIZE AND DISPLACEMENT DIFFERENCE

The five cruisers of the *Hipper* class can be subdivided into two subcategories based on size as well as appearance. *Hipper* and *Blücher* were built with a waterline length of 636ft 9in (194.2m). As designed the machinery compartments were very cramped and it was noted that the cramped conditions might interfere with crew efficiency. As a consequence it was decided to slightly lengthen and widen the design to provide more space in the machinery compartments. These spaces were lengthened from .75m to 1.25m, increasing the waterline length to 654ft 4in (199.5m). The beam was increased from 69ft 9in (21.3m) to 71ft 9in (21.9m). The new design, inaugurated with *Prinz Eugen*, rode deeper in the water with a mean draught of 20ft 9in (6.37m) compared to the 19ft (5.83m) of *Hipper* and *Blücher*. Displacement rose from 14,247 tons in *Hipper* to 16,277 tons (standard) in *Prinz Eugen*. *Seydlitz* and *Lützow* were built to the new *Prinz Eugen* hull design.

AIRCRAFT ARRANGEMENTS

The lengthening of the hull for *Prinz Eugen* also affected the external appearance of the ship, making it very easy to distinguish her from her sisters. The *Hipper* and *Blücher* had a small hangar capable of only storing one Arado seaplane. These ships carried three, one in the hangar, one on the catapult and the third stored on the hangar roof. Of course the aircraft stored outside the hangar were exposed to the elements and were very susceptible to damage in bad weather. With the extra length designers could add a longer hangar in *Prinz Eugen*, allowing two aircraft to be stored front to back, as the hangar was still narrow. The ship still carried three aircraft but at least the two in the hangar were protected from the elements. The hangar was very narrow and the wings of the Arados were stowed separately, rather than have folding wings. As a consequence, it increased the preparation time for flight operations, and in practice the Arados proved of limited value. With *Hipper* it was discovered that normal sea conditions in the North Atlantic precluded flight operations. Although the aircraft had more success in Norwegian waters, more than once an Arado was launched from *Hipper* never to be heard from again. *Prinz Eugen* enjoyed more success with her Arados but in a role for which they were not designed. In 1944 and 1945 the staple diet of *Prinz Eugen* was to provide fire support for Wehrmacht units along the Baltic coast. The Arados were used as aerial observation posts and radioed adjustments of fire. This role of the cruiser was greatly appreciated

Above: The lengthened hull of *Prinz Eugen* allowed more space for the aircraft arrangements, with an enlarged hangar sited abaft the catapult. As can be seen in this April 1941 view, the hangar was lower in the superstructure and almost invisible, compared to the prominent pitched roof of the hangar forward of the catapult in other ships of the class. Note the stripe of the ship's Baltic camouflage.

Below: *Prinz Eugen* preparing to launch an Arado 196 in the Baltic 1944. At this time the aircraft was mainly employed for artillery spotting, a role in which they were quite effective.

Above: The *Prinz Eugen*'s modified hangar housed two Arado 196 floatplanes, but only in a dismantled condition. This view of one of them being removed from the hangar, late in 1942, indicates what a time-consuming process it was to fit the wings and prepare the aircraft for flight.

Right: An Ar 196 takes to the air from *Prinz Eugen* in the Baltic 1944. The more heavily armed A-3 model replaced the A-1 from 1940 and equipped *Prinz Eugen* and *Admiral Hipper* for the rest of the war.

ARADO 196 A-3 RECONNAISSANCE FLOATPLANE CHARACTERISTICS

Maximum Speed	Ceiling	Range	Powerplant	Armament
193mph	23,000ft	670 miles	970hp BMW 132k nine-cylinder radial	Two 20mm cannon in wings; three 7.9mm MG17 machine guns, one forward and two for rear gunner: two 110lb bombs

by army commanders and it was common for *Prinz Eugen* to get thank-you notes from Wehrmacht division commanders.

The change in hangar dimensions was facilitated by changing the catapult arrangement. With *Hipper* and *Blücher* the catapult position was next to the mainmast, while the cranes were on the main deck between the catapult and funnel. The positioning of the cranes and catapult was completely rearranged for *Prinz Eugen*. The catapult was moved forward to just behind the funnel, while the cranes were also moved forward on the main deck to be placed abreast of the funnel rear face. Crane design was changed as well. For *Hipper* and *Blücher* the crane arm had a slight bent angle just behind the outward tip. For *Prinz Eugen* the crane arm was bent 45-degrees at mid-point. The crane base/machinery housing was also of a different and taller design. Concurrent with these changes there was also a minor change in the mainmast, which actually had a light tripod arrangement. With the catapult aft, next to the mainmast in *Hipper*, the wing legs of the tripod trailed aft from the centre leg and in certain conditions could restrict the field of fire of the AA guns. With *Prinz Eugen* the catapult was moved forward and the wing legs of the tripod swept forward from the centre leg, increasing the field of fire of the aft AA.

BRIDGE DIFFERENCES

As originally built the ships had two bridges with the navigation bridge behind Bruno turret and an admiral's command bridge halfway up the superstructure tower. The admiral's bridge was open to the elements and it was quickly discovered even in the mild conditions of the Baltic in midsummer, that an open bridge mounted high on the superstructure was not conducive to efficient naval staff operations. As a consequence, the Admiral's bridge was enclosed. However, there were no equipment controls on the admiral's bridge, just voice tubes for communications. This proved disadvantageous from time to time and the bridge was subsequently fitted with rudimentary controls. The appearance of the navigation

Above: Recovering the aircraft after the sortie: *Prinz Eugen*, Baltic 1944. The sea needed to be fairly calm to allow this operation, so the value of floatplanes was greatly diminished in the wider oceans.

Below: *Blücher* during working up trials in the Baltic, September 1939, shows off the bridge front as completed.

Above: *Prinz Eugen* on 27 August 1940 steaming at 32 knots during high speed trials in the Baltic. The windows of the admiral's bridge were an early modification to the class.

Right: *Prinz Eugen*: profile of the bridge structure in 1944. A 20mm *vierling* has replaced the searchlight on the platform above the admiral's bridge.

Below: *Prinz Eugen*: the back of the bridge and funnel, upper director forward with radar antenna, 1944.

Below: A close-up of one of *Prinz Eugen*'s after director cupolas, during Baltic trials, mid to late 1940. At this time the forward directors were uncovered, the cuplola housings being in short supply. A single 20mm and twin 37mm AA can also been seen in the foreground.

SUMMARY OF *ADMIRAL HIPPER* MODIFICATIONS

Date	AA Modification	Other modification
July-September 1939		*Atlantik* bow, funnel cap, modified bridge fitted
January 1940		FuMo22 radar fitted to foretop rangefinder
April 1940	Army pattern single 20mm guns added to top of B & C turrets	
September 1940		FuMO27 radar fitted to foretop and aft fire control
September 1941	Replaced searchlight with *vierling* 20mm quad on tower platform	
Feb-March 1942	Two *vierling* 20mm quad mounts replaced single 20mm on B & C turrets and another added to forecastle Two *vierling* 20mm mounts on funnel platform and 8 single 20mm guns added Replaced forward two 37mm mounts and three quad 20mm with single 40mm Bofors; single 20mm replaced with twin 20mm	
January 1945		FuMO25 added radar to mainmast

Looking aft in *Prinz Eugen* during Baltic trials, January 1941, a view dominated by the spherical AA directors. Note also the hangar roof forward of the mainmast. At this time the torpedo tube mounts apparently still have open control positions, although they were later enclosed.

SUMMARY OF *PRINZ EUGEN* MODIFICATIONS

Date	AA Modification	Other modification
1 August 1940		FuMO27 radar fitted to foretop & aft fire control
June 1941	Protective shielding added to forward pair AA directors	
December 1941	Four *vierling* 20mm quad mounts added, one each on B & C turrets, one to forecastle and one to quarterdeck	
January 1942	Another *vierling* 20mm mount replaced searchlight on foretop	
May 1942	Two *vierling* 20mm mounts on funnel platform and 8 single 20mm guns added	
September 1942		FuMO26 radar fitted to foretop
Mid 1944		FuMO25 radar fitted to mainmast; FuMO81 to foretop
September 1944	Six 40mm single Bofors, two *vierling* 20mm quads, ten 20mm twin mounts; four twin 37mm retained and the rest landed	
December 1944	All 37mm landed – fit is now eighteen 40mm single Bofors, six *vierling* 20mm quads & four 20mm twin mounts	

bridge was different in the *Hipper/Blücher* from the *Prinz Eugen*. The original tower searchlight platform had railing, which was subsequently replaced by solid splinter shielding. The searchlight disappeared when replaced by a quadruple 20mm *vierling* mount.

HIGH ANGLE DIRECTOR CUPOLAS

There were four HA anti-aircraft directors and each was given sliding spherical covers to protect the device from adverse weather. These spherical covers gave the positions the appearance of a golf ball on a tee. However, *Prinz Eugen* did not receive these

Above: Looking aft in *Hipper* during battle practice, Norway early 1942.

Above, right: A single 20mm mount with crew closed up, *Admiral Hipper* 1942. Note the crewman with a hand-held rangefinder, a very ineffective device.

Right: The funnel platform of *Hipper* with a close-up of one of the searchlights, Norway early 1942.

covers for her two forward positions, located on each side of the tower, until June 1941 after she had arrived in Brest. Therefore, when portrayed in her raid with *Bismarck*, there should be director equipment but not the spherical covers. *Bismarck* was also affected by this shortage of covers and only had her forward positions covered and not the aft two positions.

LIGHT ANTI-AIRCRAFT GUNS

As completed, the cruisers of the *Hipper* class had a remarkably heavy anti-aircraft fit. One need only compare with the AA fit of RN and USN cruisers of the same period to see the difference. As with the secondary guns in the cruiser designs from other navies, the 4.1in (105mm) guns were dual purpose DP providing heavy AA, as well as surface fire ability. For medium AA guns the Royal Navy had the 2pdr (40mm) pom-pom mount and the USN used the ineffectual 1.1in mount. For light AA defence the RN had the quad Vickers machine gun mount and the USN relied on single machine gun positions. The twin 37mm mounts of the *Hipper* class and especially the 20mm single gun light AA were a significantly more effective AA fit than the RN or USN equivalents. As the war progressed more and more light AA was provided, usually in the form of quadruple barrel 20mm mounts called *vierling*. *Hipper* was given four of these mounts between late fall 1941 and early 1942 with one mount for Bruno turret, Caesar turret, forecastle and the tower searchlight platform. *Prinz Eugen* received five *vierling* with an additional mount for the quarterdeck. Two more *vierling* were squeezed in during the spring of 1942 by replacing the searchlights on the funnel platform. The twin 37mm guns were not fully automatic and the admirals were not happy with their rate of fire. For a replacement Germany turned to the ordnance developed in another country. As a neutral, Sweden could sell war armament to both sides. The Swedish firm of Bofors did just that. The USN had purchased production rights for the excellent Bofors 40mm AA gun and the German navy purchased the same 40mm gun as a replacement for its own 37mm design. Unlike the USN, which placed the Bofors in twin or quadruple mounts, German Bofors were placed in single gun mounts. The single gun Bofors started replacing 37mm twin mounts on *Hipper* in

Above: *Prinz Eugen*'s crew at work removing 8in cartridge cases from the after turrets using a rope fender to protect the deck, Norway May 1942. In the background 4.1in and 37mm twin mounts can be seen, the main elements of the ship's AA defence.

Below: *Prinz Eugen*: twin 4.1in AA mount and director positions, Baltic trials, mid to late 1940.

Opposite, left: *Prinz Eugen*: view of fore and mainmast at commissioning, 1 August 1940 – devoid of any electronics except radio aerials.

spring 1942 and for *Prinz Eugen* there was wholesale replacement of the 37mm guns by 1944. To increase light AA fire, single 20mm guns were replaced by twin gun mounts.

RADAR ARRAYS

By 1940 the *Hipper* class cruisers had effective radar but with limitations. All three ships to see service were initially equipped with two FuMO27 arrays, one on top of the tower and the other on the aft fire control station. These were large rectangular mattress arrays of 2 metres by 4 metres. These early sets were very prone to being disabled by the concussion of the firing of the cruisers' own guns. The FuMO26 replaced the FuMO27 in 1942 in *Prinz Eugen*. The FuMO26 added further aerials for air detection. The FuMO25 was of the same size as the other two but was more accurate. FuMO25 was placed on the mainmast of *Prinz Eugen* in 1944 and probably *Hipper* did so as well in her preparation for active service in 1944.

Prinz Eugen's after director with FuMO27 radar array, 1944.

OTHER DIFFERENCES

Both *Hipper* and *Blücher* had open control platforms on their torpedo mounts. Torpedo mounts open to the weather in the Baltic in winter would have a detrimental effect on the crew manning the weapon system. Accordingly, the torpedo mounts on *Prinz Eugen* were given a lightly armoured closed position, which greatly improved crew conditions. When the 105mm gun was designed, the existing twin 88mm mount was selected as a temporary mounting until a purpose-built twin mount was developed. The modified 88mm mount was designated 8.8cm Dopp.L. C/31, while the ordnance-specific mount was designated Dopp.L. C/37. The first three cruisers all received the earlier mount but *Seydlitz* received the Dopp.L. C/37. An external degaussing cable to reduce the cruiser's magnetic signature was added to the ships in 1940.

CAMOUFLAGE SCHEMES

As completed, Admiral *Hipper*, *Blücher* and *Prinz Eugen* were finished in overall light grey. However, two different types of grey paint were used. The paint used for the hull was slightly darker than that used for the superstructure. *Hipper* was an early recipient of a light grey/dark grey splinter camouflage designed to break up the ship's profile. Initially received in spring 1940, the pattern changed in early 1942 in her deployment to Norway. When laid up after the Battle of Barents Sea, the paint as well as the fabric of the ship were allowed to deteriorate. Then in 1944 when it was decided to bring *Hipper* back into service, dark grey splotches were added to the splinter camouflage pattern, with the splotches appearing on the superstructure and at the very top of the hull. *Blücher* with such a short life, never received a camouflage scheme. In trials *Prinz Eugen*, along

Hipper crewmen working on the open control position of the triple torpedo mount in 1940, during the invasion of Norway.

Above: *Prinz Eugen*: view of mainmast from below, 1944. The ship does not seem to have yet acquired the FuMO25 aerial on the mainmast platform.

Below: Taken in 1946 at Boston, this close-up of *Prinz Eugen* shows single 40mm AA mounts atop B turret and on deck just abaft it.

SUMMARY OF *ADMIRAL HIPPER* CAMOUFLAGE PATTERNS

Date	Location	Pattern
April 1939	Trials	Light grey overall
April 1940	*Operation Weserübung* – Norway	Light grey overall with carmine turret crowns
June – Early 1941	Norway	Overall light grey with multiple dark grey bars, green starboard half of A & B turret crowns as well as port AA director shielding
Early 1942 – Early 1943	Norway – Battle of Barents Sea	Overall light grey; dark grey rays
Early 1944	Germany – Baltic	Overall light grey with dark grey irregular bars, superstructure had mixture of dark grey bars and dapple

SUMMARY OF *PRINZ EUGEN* CAMOUFLAGE PATTERNS

Date	Location	Pattern
August 1940	Baltic	Overall grey at commissioning and start of trials – carmine turret crowns
March-May 1941	Baltic	Bar camouflage with black and white stripes on hull and superstructure sides; swastika aerial recognition panels on forecastle and quarterdeck; carmine or wine red turret crowns
May 22, 1941	Grimstadfjord, Norway	Hull stripes over-painted light grey in preparation for Atlantic sortie – turret crowns repainted overall grey
Summer 1941 to February 1942	Brest, France	Light grey with dark grey bow & stern and multiple stripes, dark grey dapples on superstructure - carmine turret crowns
May 16-18, 1942	Kiel, Germany	Light grey with dark grey bow, stern and waterline panel connecting bow and stern portions, carmine crowns
1943-1945	Baltic Operations	Lower third of hull dark grey with upper two-thirds of hull and superstructure light grey with carmine turret crowns

Right: *Admiral Hipper* carrying a recognition swastika on the forecastle, sometime in late 1940 or early 1941.

Below: *Prinz Eugen* boat crane amidships, Baltic trials, mid to late 1940.

with *Bismarck*, received the unique white and black diagonal stripe design used in the Baltic in the spring of 1941. Ships in the Baltic were given dark red turret crowns for aerial recognition by the Luftwaffe. When venturing into the North Atlantic the red was over-painted as any aircraft encountered was far more likely to be British. *Prinz Eugen* and *Bismarck* had their stripes painted over in Norway the day before leaving on their raid. After reaching Brest following the raid, the *Prinz Eugen* was given

In *Prinz Eugen* the torpedo tube mount was modified to provide an enclosed control position to protect the crew from bad weather. This view was taken in June 1946 at Bikini Atoll.

Prinz Eugen's crew touch up her camouflage paint some time late in 1941.

Top: Camouflage on the *Hipper*'s forward turrets, sometime in 1942-43.

Above: *Hipper*'s 11-metre motor launch in Kiel harbour, 1939. This boat type was common to all large German warships.

Above, right: *Hipper*'s 8.5-metre 10-oared cutter in Kiel harbour, 1939. This type was also to be found on all German major warships.

Right: After her return from the *Rheinübung* operation *Prinz Eugen* was the subject of frequent British air attacks at Brest in late 1941. The ship is shown here in drydock under heavy camouflage netting; note also the dappled camouflage on the AA director cupolas.

Opposite, below: Flying the US flag, the *Prinz Eugen* arrives in Boston, USA, early in 1946. The ship is noticeably light and trimmed by the stern, but still carrying her final radar configuration: FuMO26 on the main foretop director and a FuMO25 antenna on the mainmast platform.

a false bow/stern pattern in which the bow and stern were dark grey while the body of the ship was light grey with false cutwater and stern profile. Numerous dark grey bands were also added to the hull and dark grey splotches for all upper works. Turret crowns again became dark red. For the Channel Dash the hull was mostly dark grey with a light grey rectangle running from below Bruno to just aft of Caesar turret and a light grey superstructure. From 1943 to the end of the war, the scheme of *Prinz Eugen* was greatly simplified with a narrow dark grey panel at the waterline to about a third the way up the hull, running from bow to stern. The upper two-thirds of the hull and all superstructure was light grey and turret crowns carmine or dark red. White Ensign Models produces an excellent line of paints specifically mixed to match the Kriegsmarine colours. Called Colourcoats their German Kriegsmarine line provides the most exacting match commercially available for the camouflage schemes of the *Hipper* class.

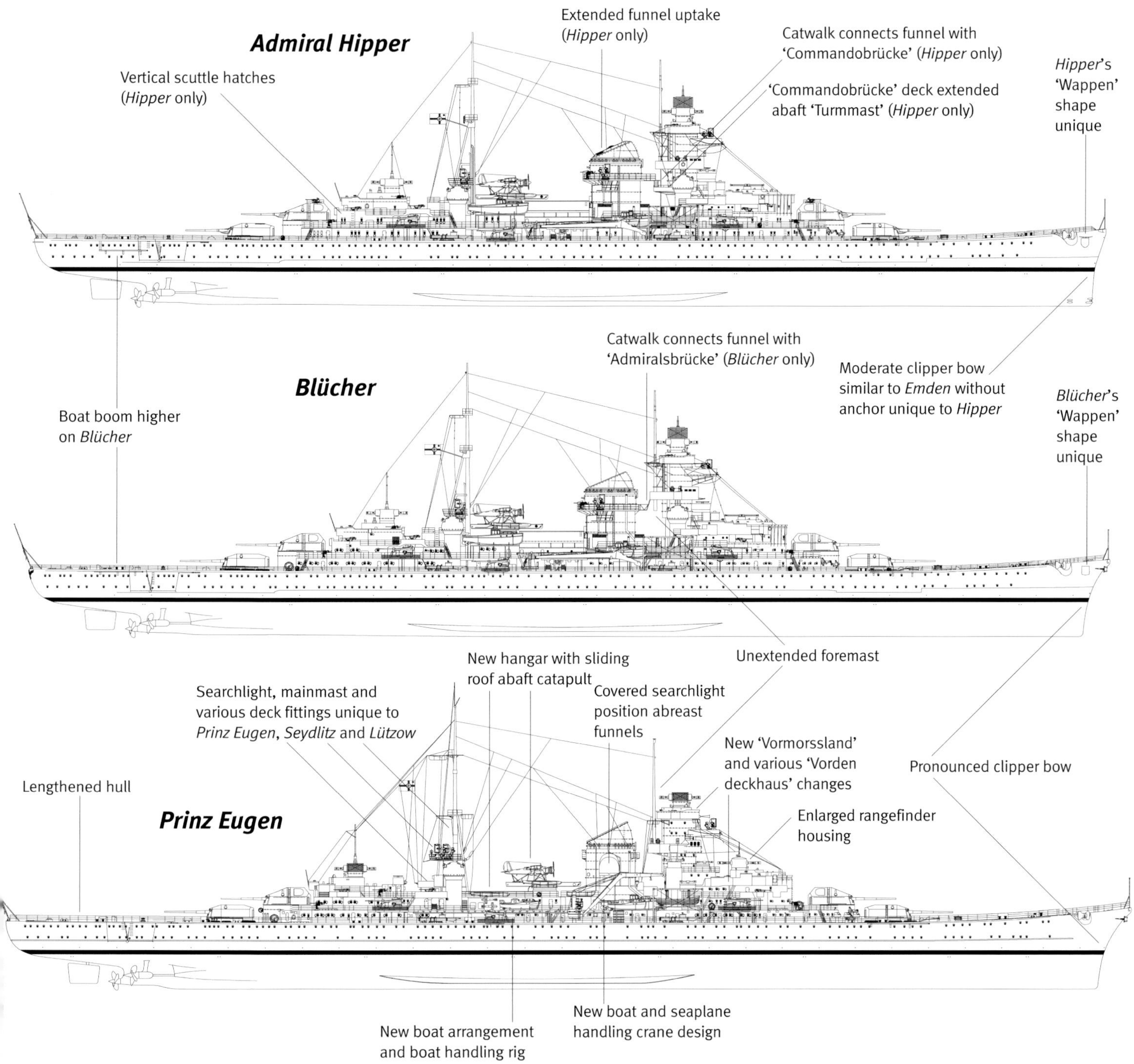
Admiral Hipper
Extended funnel uptake (Hipper only)
Catwalk connects funnel with 'Commandobrücke' (Hipper only)
Vertical scuttle hatches (Hipper only)
'Commandobrücke' deck extended abaft 'Turmmast' (Hipper only)
Hipper's 'Wappen' shape unique
Catwalk connects funnel with 'Admiralsbrücke' (Blücher only)
Moderate clipper bow similar to Emden without anchor unique to Hipper
Blücher
Boat boom higher on Blücher
Blücher's 'Wappen' shape unique
New hangar with sliding roof abaft catapult
Unextended foremast
Searchlight, mainmast and various deck fittings unique to Prinz Eugen, Seydlitz and Lützow
Covered searchlight position abreast funnels
New 'Vormorssland' and various 'Vorden deckhaus' changes
Pronounced clipper bow
Lengthened hull
Prinz Eugen
Enlarged rangefinder housing
New boat and seaplane handling crane design
New boat arrangement and boat handling rig

Selected References

BOOKS

Brzezinski, Slawomir & Moscinski Jerzy, *Admiral Hipper*, Wydawniczo-Handlown (Wyszkow, Poland 2002). Volume 50 in the prolific Profile Morskie series is just on *Admiral Hipper*. For those unfamiliar with the series, each volume has Polish text with a moderate selection of photographs but emphasises detailed line drawings on the subject. This monograph is 40 pages in length with 12 pages of photographs and 24 pages of line drawings. Most drawings are in 1:200 scale with a few in 1:100 and 1:50 scale. Also included are three separate sheets of plans with profile and plan from 1941, deck, schematic hull lines in 1:400 scale, more equipment details in 1:200 scale and a colour plate of *Hipper* in 1941 with colour guide.

Hervieux, Pierre, 'The Heavy Cruiser *Admiral Hipper* at War', *Warship Volume IX* , Conway Maritime Press (London 1985). *Hipper* has not missed an appearance in the venerable *Warship* series. The article covers eight pages and concentrates on the ship's operational career.

Koop, Gerhard & Scholke, Klaus-Peter, *Heavy Cruisers of the Admiral Hipper Class*, Greenhill Books (London 2001). Originally published in Germany in 1992, this English-language edition, translated by Geoffrey Brooks, provides 202 pages solely on the five ships of the *Hipper* class. This volume and the Whitley volume on German cruisers are the two best sources of information on the class with the AJ Press three-volume series the best for photographs and graphics.

Perepeczko. Andrzej, *Niemieckie Krazowniki Admiral Hipper CZ.1* (Heavy Cruiser Type *Admiral Hipper* Part One), Volume 33 Encyklopedia Okretow Wojennych, AJ Press (Gdansk, Poland 2003). This is the first in a three-volume series on the *Hipper* class cruisers, all volumes providing a superb source of excellent photographs, 3-view drawings and colour profiles and plan views. Volume 33 covers the design, construction, trials, equipment and systems of the class. Text is in Polish and English in 64 pages. Detailed additional inserted plans cover:

Sheet One – Plan & Profile of the 1936 light cruiser design for *Seydlitz* and *Lützow*; hull lines, body plan, hull profile and plan for *Hipper*; *Lützow* plan and profile when transferred to the Soviet Union, all drawings in 1:400 scale.
Sheet Two – Plans and profiles for *Hipper* April 1939, November 1939 and March 1941 and *Blücher* September 1939, in 1:400 scale.
Sheet Three – Nine CGI drawings of the superstructure of *Hipper*.
Sheet Four – continues CGI coverage with another ten drawings of *Hipper*'s superstructure.
Sheet Five – Colour starboard and port profiles and plan of *Hipper* with Norwegian camouflage, starboard profiles of *Prinz Eugen* in Baltic trial camouflage, early *Operation Rheinübung* camouflage (Baltic stripes), and late *Operation Rheinübung* camouflage, 1:400 scale.
Sheet Six – Plan and profile drawings in 1:400 scale for *Seydlitz* as carrier *Weser*, *Prinz Eugen* minus stern February 1942, and *Prinz Eugen* May 1945.

Perepeczko. Andrzej, *Niemieckie Krazowniki Admiral Hipper CZ.2* (Heavy Cruiser Type *Admiral Hipper* Part Two), Volume 34 Encyklopedia Okretow Wojennych, AJ Press. (Gdansk, Poland 2004). Volume 34 covers the operations of the class up to spring 1941. Text in Polish and English in 64 pages. Superb additional inserted plans cover:

Sheet Seven – The entire sheet consists of very detailed drawings of *Hipper* platforms, superstructure levels and equipment in 1:200 scale.
Sheet Eight – continues with the 1:200 scale drawings but concentrates on superstructure sections with emphasis on the hangar, funnel and Arado aircraft.Sheet Nine – a series of 14 beautifully rendered CGI illustrations of the main gun turrets of *Hipper* and *Prinz Eugen*.
Sheet Ten – examines the 105mm, 37mm and 20mm single mounts with another 28 CGI illustrations.

Perepeczko. Andrzej, *Niemieckie Krazowniki Admiral Hipper CZ.3* (Heavy Cruiser Type *Admiral Hipper* Part Three), Volume 35 Encyklopedia Okretow Wojennych, AJ Press (Gdansk, Poland 2005). Volume 35 covers the operations of the class from spring 1941 to the end of the war. Text in Polish and English in 64 pages. Superb additional inserted plans.

Schmalenbach, Paul, *Kreuzer Prinz Eugen Unter Drei Flaggen*, Koehlers Verlagsgesellschaft (Hamburg 1998). If you cannot get enough of the glamorous *Prinz Eugen*, this book is for you. The author was the gunnery officer of the ship from August 1940 to March 1945 and he supplies 226 pages of the obvious and obscure – but it is entirely in German. The volume is mostly text but with a fair number of photographs.

Schmalenbach, Paul, *Warships in Profile, Volume 1, KM Prinz Eugen*, Profile Publications Ltd (Windsor 1973). The monograph on the *Prinz Eugen* was first published separately in softbound format as Profile 6 and then incorporated in the hardbound yearly compilation of the 'Warships in Profile' titles. The monograph is 24 pages in length and provides a good mixture of text and photographs. The two-page colour profile and plan is the centrefold of the volume shows the Baltic black and white stripe pattern but without the carmine turret crowns.

Whitley, M. J., *German Cruisers of World War Two*, Naval Institute Press (Annapolis, Maryland 1985). With this volume of 176 pages devoted to the handful of cruisers produced by Germany before World War Two the reader is rewarded with extensive coverage of the *Hipper* class. The title also benefits from extensive use of photographs, charts and drawings.

Wiper, Steve, *Kriegsmarine Prinz Eugen, Warship Pictorial 21*, Classic Warships Publishing (Tucson, Arizona 2006). As the title indicates this volume is a pictorial survey of the *Prinz Eugen*. The format emphasises the use of clear, excellent photographs on high quality glossy stock with comprehensive captions to illustrate the features of a particular ship. There are 72 pages of photographs showing overall portraits of the ship as well as many detailed shots of armament, fittings and equipment. It provides ideal coverage for the modeller.

WEBSITES OF CONTRIBUTORS

www.classicwarships.com
www.collectableships.com
www.flyhawkmodel.com
www.freetimehobbies.com
www.jsc.pl
www.larsenal.com/
www.lionroar.net
www.navis-neptun.de
www.pacificfront.com
www.voyagermodel.com
www.whiteensignmodels.com

OTHER WEBSITES OF INTEREST

www.bismarck-class.dk/index.html
www.feldgrau.com/kriegs.html
www.german-navy.de/kriegsmarine/index.html
www.kbismarck.com
www.kriegsmarine-reich.co.uk
www.modelwarship.com
www.prinzeugen.com
www.steelnavy.com
www.youtube.com/watch?v=eLtAFDRveGo [Jonathan Bird's Blue World #10- Exploring the Prinz Eugen]